STRATEGIES FOR CHANGE

STRATEGIES FOR CHANGE:
THE FUTURE OF FRENCH SOCIETY

MICHEL CROZIER
translated by
William R. Beer

The MIT Press
Cambridge, Massachusetts
London, England

Originally published in France under the title *On ne change pas la société par décret,* by Bernard Grasset, Inc., 1979.

This book was set in Meridien by Achorn Graphic Services and printed and bound in the United States of America.

Library of Congress Cataloging in Publication Data

Crozier, Michel.
  Strategies for change.

  Translation of: On ne change pas la société par décret.
  Includes bibliographical references.
  1. France—Social conditions.   2. France—Social policy.   I. Title.
HN430.C7513   944.08   81-20805
ISBN 0-262-03082-9   AACR2

CONTENTS

FOREWORD

There are two ways of reading this book, and both are right. It can, in the first place, be read as Michel Crozier's fourth attempt to diagnose the French "bureaucratic phenomenon" and to suggest ways of transforming it. In the classic work by that title, published in 1964, he had described the traditional and resilient French style of authority relations, with its fear of face-to-face confrontations, its preference for the resolution of conflicts by higher authority, its mania for rules and regulations protecting people in each stratum from higher authority as well as from one another, its vertical and horizontal stratification, its innumerable *blocages* of information and action, and also its "behind the counter" networks of clandestine accommodation and negotiations. Later empirical studies by Crozier and his able team of associates made it possible to understand in some detail how this model of centralized authority actually worked in concrete cases, such as France's system of territorial government, or government-business relations. *The Stalled Society* (published in France in 1970) examined in particular the spectacular crisis of 1968 in the light of Crozier's theory and showed how the French university system had carried both the "bureaucratic phenomenon" and *blocage* to the point of explosion.

Actors and Systems (published in France in 1977), co-authored by Erhard Friedberg, is Crozier's most ambitious theoretical effort so far. It contains both a kind of balance sheet of the empirical research undertaken during a quarter of a century by Crozier and his collaborators and a new model, that of a strategy for social change. It is based on his conviction that the very complexity of modern societies, which dooms the traditional French style of authority to inefficiency and French citizens to frustration as long as this style persists, increases the opportunities for individual and group action available to each citizen. Yet people are often, and instinctively, afraid of responsibility and choice and still prefer being able to blame an outside force for its mistakes—and for their troubles—to endorsing full responsibility for their own decisions. The method of change Crozier recommends could be called the art of training people for choice. Their freedom and choices will expand if they first learn the "rules of the game," or rather games, that make up any society. Rather than begin with grand ideological theories and lofty goals, we should start with an effort to understand the "concrete systems" in which we operate and try to develop what he calls institutional investment—investments in knowledge, in human efforts, in social experiments, aimed at changing traditional behavior and at promoting individual and group initiative, not by destroying the organizations in which people in modern societies work but by transforming them. Crozier is a voluntarist, but also a realist. Change is necessary and possible, but not *any* change and not everywhere at once: Crozier's sociology is strictly anti-utopian, precisely because he fears that attempts to enforce utopias invariably crush freedom.

The present book applies this theory to the case of France today and suggests that change be undertaken, not by direct attack on the most resistant structures (such as the university system or the secondary schools, or the central administrations) but by a reform of less formidable or weaker institutions situated at such strategic points that their transformation would have effects throughout French society: local government, the *Grandes Ecoles*, the research system. Also, since the development of human initiative is the objective of the whole effort, Crozier insists on the need to free French enterprises from the weight of external regulations and internal barriers to efficiency—from what he calls the bureaucratic effect and the eiderdown effect.

The second way of reading this book is to see it as an attempt by citizen Michel Crozier—informed by his experience and reflections as a sociologist—to have his say in the French political debate of the mid and late 1970s. In 1974, Valéry Giscard d'Estaing had been elected president on a promise of change; he was, he suggested, going to fulfill the hopes which Prime Minister Jacques Chaban-Delmas's famous speech of September 1969, denouncing the stalled society, had raised, but which President Pompidou had squashed. Giscard, in his own book *French Democracy* (1977), outlined—rather sketchily—a program of "advanced liberalism," which owed much to Tocqueville and Crozier. At the same time, Socialists and Communists, in the Common Program of 1972, concentrated their attacks on the multiple inequalities and iniquities of French society and suggested rather traditional Leftist remedies that included more state regulation and more nationalizations, while many Socialists and trade unionists devised schemes for workers' control or *autogestion*.

Crozier's book is both a sharp critique of the Left's ideas and an implicit criticism of Giscard's actions. The Left, as he sees it, remains either too deeply enamored of bureaucratic solutions and security, too suspicious of private enterprise, initiative, and profit, or else too fond of the dream of total harmony—not the resolution of inevitable conflicts through compromise but their disappearance by a sudden fusion of wills: a dream that often led Leftist *groupuscules* to admire totalitarian schemes and leads, in practice, regularly, to the stifling of individual efforts by group pressure, to group manipulation by minorities, and to control by central power. But—except with respect to industry, where Prime Minister Raymond Barre, especially after the victory of the Right at the legislative elections of March 1978, enforced a policy of price deregulation and tried (although with the usual bureaucratic means) to encourage competitiveness and profitability—most of the changes Crozier describes here as possible and important were not undertaken by President Giscard. Under his rule, regional reform was abandoned; never did the *Grands Corps* dominate French administration more and the *Grandes Ecoles* benefit more from the state's determination to curb the limited autonomy universities had achieved after 1968; and neither in the firms nor at the national level did the system of industrial relations conform to Crozier's wishes.

The specific liberal tradition to which he belongs has always been in a difficult situation in France. It is too hostile to centralization and to the state's claim of a monopoly on the public interest to please the heirs of the Jacobins, too anti-elitist to please the conservatives, too determined to put individual opportunities ahead of equality and free initiative ahead of regulation to please the Left. It is not by coincidence that Tocqueville, Raymond Aron, and Crozier have had to criticize relentlessly both the complacency of the Right in power and the illusions of the Left in opposition. Tocqueville, who had warned the July Monarchy about the perils of immobility and who wanted to reconcile democracy and liberty, nevertheless chose reaction and the "party of order"—i.e., a restriction of liberty and a leap away from democracy—when, in the Spring of 1848, it seemed to him that there was only a choice between such reaction and an unliberal, leveling socialism. Aron, concerned above all with economic efficiency in a liberal capitalist society and skeptical about the chances or benefits of widespread social change, has also chosen the Right over the Left.

In the presidential elections of 1981, in circumstances far less dramatic than those faced by Tocqueville, Crozier endorsed Giscard against Mitterrand. He appears to have believed that the policies of the Left would make the scope and weight of the

French state even deadlier, wipe out the gains in efficiency and competitiveness made by French enterprises, and restrict the opportunities for experimentation and social change *à la base* which had, in the past thirty years and despite the "bureaucratic phenomenon," deeply transformed many of France's sectors and forces, such as agriculture or the Catholic Church. The risk of state immobilism, in case of a reelection of Giscard, must have seemed to Crozier less dangerous (as long as it was coupled with a program of economic liberalization) than the obsolete or utopian models and hazardous Keynesian economic program of the Left. The truth of the matter is that there was not, on the French political scene, any Crozerian leader: neither Mitterrand nor Giscard, certainly not Chirac, and probably not Rocard. It is also true that, in recent years, Crozier has become increasingly doubtful about social change promoted from above, as his sharp critique of American liberalism in his latest book shows (*Le mal américain,* 1980); and he was increasingly optimistic about piecemeal changes initiated far from, and far below, the state. The Right's political and social forces, whatever their blind spots, seemed to him more modern, or modernizing, and leff stifling, than those of the Left.

And yet Mitterrand got elected—with the help of the very social forces that the profound transformation of French society into an urban society of wage earners had engendered; and the Socialists now control the French state. The weakening of the Communist party, the statist bureaucratic party par excellence, should allay some of Crozier's fears. One of the reforms Crozier has most insistently argued for—drastic decentralization, focused on the regions—is likely to be carried out by the new government. Many of its other announced measures, such as a new series of nationalizations and the hiring of more civil servants, are not likely to win Crozier's favor. The struggle within the Socialist party between those whose views come closer to Crozier's and the traditional statist social-democrats, or Marxist anti-capitalists, or technocrats, has not been resolved. Unemployment—an issue not discussed in his book, which turned out to be fatal to Giscard and Barre, and which the Socialists want to fight in ways that could be inflationary and nefarious for French competitiveness in the world economy—is likely to remain more salient a social issue than some of the topics addressed here by Crozier. Yet in the long run, however debatable his own political choices or however uncomfortable his position along the French political spectrum may be, the issues he has raised here are the decisive ones for any person interested in seeing French society meet the "challenge of complexity" in a way that fosters individual initiative and collective experimentation.

At a moment when French intellectuals appear to have moved away, as Crozier had hoped they would, from the attraction of total change and the illusion of serving as the guides and consciences of their time, but often at the cost of repudiating political concerns altogether, taking refuge instead either in esoteric research, or in noisy and biased forays into history for the purpose of settling old accounts and of satisfying the media's insatiable need for excitement, Crozier's book is a fine example of responsible and enlightened thought. To the American reader, two years after its publication in France, it can serve as a yardstick for assessing both the late Giscard government and the new French Socialist regime—and as a model of applied sociology.

Stanley Hoffmann

STRATEGIES FOR CHANGE

1

THE CRISIS OF WESTERN SOCIETY

Every Society Is a Complex System

We will never succeed in changing society the way we want. Even if we were to persuade the majority of our fellow citizens to follow our lead, we would not succeed in enacting a plan for society because society, human relations, and social systems are too complex. We would have succeeded in mobilizing nothing but an abstract and unsubstantial agreement, the awakened dreams of our fellow men. This desire, this fantasy, never determines how people really act.

It is possible to work within a system only by understanding its characteristics. This assertion is not as self-evident as it may appear because all too often we are not willing to understand society as it is. Instead we spend our time making social blueprints that do not have the slightest chance of success because they do not take into account the complex working of human relationships and everyday social interaction.

Every society is a complex system, and this is why it cannot be changed or renewed simply by a decision, even one arrived at democratically by majority rule. This is not to say that there are fixed laws of society, imposed on humanity like a sort of divine will. This all-too-human construction is the product of human history, and so it can be shaped, reworked, and changed. But at the same time it is a system, an interdependent framework of relations that is beyond the conscious will of individual people.

Of course, neither these relations nor the whole system are unalterable. They do change as a result of human action, but the overall result of this action is different from the wishes of individual people. It is possible to bring about change more consciously and effectively, but it is not possible to impose a specific program simply through the agreement of individual people. This may seem contradictory, particularly if the profound difference that exists between people's individual preferences and their real behavior toward others is not appreciated.

Behavior in social relationships is like a game in which each person depends on the other. To win, or simply not to lose, you have to take the possible reactions of others into account. The games of social life make us obey rules that are independent of us. These games are regulated, commanded, corrected, and maintained by mechanisms to which we do not have direct access. These games are the building blocks of systems that organize every one of our activities, including the biggest and most complex, society itself.

When a warehouse worker sets aside a special supply of goods to meet unexpected requests of production workers, while at the same time politely refusing to provide for the maintenance workers, he is neither obeying his boss nor hoping for the final victory of the working class. It is not because of some personal character trait that he is easy-going with his old assistant and strict with his new one. This is the only way he can succeed in keeping the wheels turning in the department that is his world of work, while at the same time keeping the respect of his peers and influencing events that affect him. This is as true at the level of society as it is at the level of a business.

Games, systems, and society are the necessary mediators of all human action, but they are structured in such a way that this mediation can have an effect opposite to what most participants want or think they want. The road to hell, as everyone knows, is paved with good intentions. To set up the rule of virtue, hypocrisy and eavesdropping are brought in, and have been from the time of Savonarola to Mao; the control of excess profits strengthens the black market. And very often in the attempt to free people, new chains are forged for them. Every organized human action, every collective effort and even ideological movements lead to what can be called the perverse effect, effects that are the opposite of what the participants wanted. These perverse effects cannot be blamed on some force of evil—neither on the powerful at the top of the social scale nor on agitators at the bottom. They are the necessary consequence of interdependent relationships among people.

This will come as a surprise to those who still believe in the myth of the social contract, believing that the collective will of people, the sum of their individual wishes, naturally produces rational decisions. The use of opinion polls has given new respectability and weight to this idealistic view of democracy. In fact, we are prisoners of our social situation, of our relationships, of our need to exist for, with, and against other people. Outside of this situation and these interactions, we cannot decide what we want because we literally do not know. This is why abstract opinion, cut off from the real context of social relations, only partially indicates what our real behavior is. In the spring of 1968, opinion polls registered satisfaction in France, and the pollsters said that the students had never been so happy.[1]

It would be tempting to conclude that it is better not to try to intervene at all since every social action leads to a series of effects that can be the exact opposite of what was intended. This is the temptation of pessimism that has recently reappeared among the "new philosophers." It must be resisted, not simply because it leads people to give up but also because it leads to an even worse state of affairs. Every situation in which we do not intervene tends to deteriorate. Every analysis of businesses or institutions that are not working reveals that the same rules and principles that were successful twenty or thirty years ago are the cause of disorder and failure today.

So it is not a question of choosing between action and retreat but of finding the means and direction of the action that cannot be avoided. In everyday life, we continually make choices on the basis of tested rules based on our experience. Unfortunately we cannot transpose this principle to a broader area because individually we are helpless against large-scale organizations, nationwide societies, and the world order. The inescapable recognition of our limitations leads us to examine two principles of action.

The first principle is that of giving priority to the understanding of real systems, not to the discussion of aims and ideals. We can find out what we want only if we know what we are doing. As long as we are not aware of what is really going on, our ideals and goals are nothing but projections of our inadequacies and inabilities. We can progress only by bringing the ideal back to earth, by putting the system of relations on its feet: reality first, ideals later.

The second principle, a consequence of understanding the perverse effect, is that we have to get away from the guesswork of everyday activity. We have to spend as much energy on the ongoing operation of the system as we do on utopian projects for changing the whole system radically and idealistically. We cannot do our job as responsible people and citizens unless we go beyond the sort of blind empiricism that led an English minister of foreign affairs to declare shortly before the war in 1914, "You know, nothing really ever happens."

We Live in the Midst of an Explosion of Human Relations

The fact that society is a complex system prevents us from intervening in an idealistic way, but the fact that it is a system that naturally tends to deteriorate requires that we intervene. To resolve this contradiction, we have to deepen our diagnosis by going beyond a mere listing of deadly social ills that must be cured to an analysis of the constraints we must respect and the real problems to be solved.

At present the diagnosis that underlies the reformist or revolutionary beliefs that are prevalent in the West appears to focus on threats to the individual. The individual is supposed to be oppressed by machines, alienated by a consumer society, and overwhelmed by the sheer size of organizations. I would like to declare my disagreement with this diagnosis, which I do not think is in agreement with the facts. Actually the average citizen has never been so free in his range of choices as he is now and has never been able to exert so much influence when grouped together with others as he currently can. People obviously are not all powerful and do not have the unlimited autonomy needed to bring about the utopian states they dream about. But they have much more power in other everyday practices of social life than they think. They either do not know how much they have or do not want to know so that they can keep complaining or dreaming. If this is so, why are there all these contradictions and complaints that we hear so much about? Because we are living in the midst of an explosion of human relations. The collective features of all modern societies have in common the multiplication of the number of people with whom we interact and the increase in the complexity of our social interaction. These changes are the result of a trend that has been studied in the past and is accelerating today: the growth in the number of relationships among people. In a way this growth is the essence of social development, of what used to be called civilization.

Immigrants from Eastern Europe or from developing countries are aware of the difference immediately. Coming from countries where the rhythm of life is slower, where human relationships are far fewer and far less free, they have a hard time coping with Westerners' whirlwind of activity. Europeans had the same impression of acceleration when they visited the United States thirty years ago. And if our forefathers from the early 1900s were suddenly transported to our time, they would be seized with panic.

This overall social trend has great momentum and is probably irresistible. It is composed of two parallel movements that are inextricably intertwined but are of different natures and rhythms. One increases the number of relations among social actors, the number of concrete social interactions. The other leads to an explosion of the means of communication, to an overload of messages, information, and symbols.

The multiplication of the number of social interactions is a general phenomenon, but the more general it is, the less it is noticed. What is particularly forgotten is the consequence for human beings. The exchange of goods requires the interaction of people and beyond a certain threshold leads to tension and qualitative changes in this interaction. We pay little attention to it because we get used to these changes and explain crises by other means. But if we step back for a minute, it is clear that the quantity and quality of social interactions have greatly changed in the course of history. If a person in a big business or administration were to keep a diary and record all of his contacts in the course of a single day, the importance of these interactions, with all their subtleties of manner, would be recognized. The same is true outside of organized institutions, where there is even more freedom of choice.

Each of us interacts with a much larger number of people than ever before, and with a freer choice of how and with whom we interact. There are fewer and fewer barriers to human relations, and we are not only able to have an extraordinary number of experiences more easily but we can also change partners much more easily. If we so desire, this makes us much freer in our relationships.

These statements may come as a surprise to people who complain about the lack of choice in our system. True, freedom is subjective; a person can feel free within a prison and feel a prisoner outside. But objective analysis shows that people's real choices have enormously increased at both the bottom and the top of the social ladder. This is so not only for consumer items but for knowledge of the world, choice of friends, of spouse, of career, and residence as well. Things are certainly not better, but they are open and easy.

People who have many alternatives cannot be controlled, directed, and confined in the same way as in a social system where there are far fewer possibilities. It could be argued that in fact people benefit very little from this abstract freedom, and that they interact with fewer people and in ways that are less free than they could be. In fact, people have only relatively limited physical and mental capacities and must choose what they can usefully pay attention to. But whatever the problems, the proliferation of choices makes for freedom of initiative great enough to triumph over the system. The individual cannot make himself a new world, but he can get around direct pressures on himself, and to do this he can get around the controls of the system. The system, in turn, becomes much less predictable because its old rules lose their effectiveness. The social actors have become much too free for the simplistic rules that used to work.

The explosion of communications is another aspect of the same trend. In this area, the change is even less gradual. The de-

velopment of new means of communication, their instantane-
ousness, the general explosion of the quantity and quality of
messages transmitted, have all radically changed a system in
which there used to be some limits. From now on the traditional
means for communicating information are no longer applicable,
in all institutions as well as in the whole administrative and
political system. The number of messages broadcast and available
is gigantic, and people are drowning in too much information.
The networks that select, broadcast, and shape information play a
greater and greater role, and their importance makes the regulation of systems even more complicated.[2]

It has often been observed that the image projected by the
media frequently becomes more important than action and that
people no longer try to accomplish things but to project a certain
image. The activity of the media is particularly important because
the means of communication they bring to bear is extremely dis-
ruptive. Communication by the media is emotional communication. It makes viewers react immediately and without perspective
to an event, presented as a spectacle. The portrayal of collective
behavior by the media is highly selective and is often quite dis-
torted. Here again, we are in the realm of perverse effects. Because
the media focus attention on a horrible crime, public opinion
demands the retention or the reimposition of the death penalty.
When a spectacular demonstration by a group with only a small
following gets television coverage, public opinion tends to sym-
pathize with the people who were its heroes or victims. This is
not an attack on French television alone. This sort of thing is
common in all Western television systems, public as well as
private.

Paradoxically the dispersed and fragmented world of the past
seems to have been well ordered, while today's world of concentration and interdependence seems much more confused. Actually our real problem is one of confusion and complexity, not

oppression, because our actions no longer produce results. Instead the opposite effects multiply. We no longer understand the mechanisms of social life, and we are overwhelmed by a system that seems to have become unmanageable. This feeling is probably exaggerated, but the cumulative increase of complexity caused by the rapidity of economic and social progress has in fact moved us beyond a certain threshold.

Therefore our problem is how to develop new means of control and government that can be substituted for the traditional means. And it is more important to create a new capability for action than to choose objectives that may be good in themselves but, through our inability to act, are impossible to achieve. The capability for action can neither be created nor maintained simply by returning to the old ways that preceded the crisis. Any regression toward authoritarian ways of governing is doomed from the start. But the illusions of the ultrademocratic Left are not the solution either. We can progress only by examining the social relations of today. It is particularly important that our examination take place in the context of real human institutions where it is needed—a business, a school, or a hospital, for instance—and that we analyze and understand the practical problems that are present.

Every social system is autonomous and unique, but all are subject to the same pressures. The economic growth of the past three decades has led to a disproportionate increase in the complexity of human relations and decision-making systems. At the same time, it has led to a partial breakdown of the means of social control, particularly of the agencies that manage contradictions and conflicts. Society instinctively reacts by spontaneously creating certain ways of coping with this problem, but the means available for governing social systems and decision making have decreased at the very moment when individuals' demands have grown. This has led to malaise, crises, and the risk of a return to the bad old days. The societies of Western Europe are particularly vulnerable because they have undergone a greater growth in an institutional framework that has not adapted. The countries that have been the least affected are those that were forced to transform their institutional models radically because of their defeat in 1945, Germany and Japan.

Our Institutional Means for Coping with Complexity Are Weak and Are Becoming More So

It is often said that generals fight by using the tactics of the previous war. This is true not just of warfare. A generation commonly struggles with problems that are long out of date, smashing at will through doors already opened by previous generations. This seems to me to be so with the structures of authority. These lofty priests that Buñuel, like so many other directors, keeps on making fun of in his films hardly exist any more except in the imagination. Where are the judges, professors, foremen, sergeants, and bourgeois of the past, who used to be so certain of their rectitude and so capable of commanding and imposing their will? I see only bureaucrats and middlemen who make excuses and pass the buck. Where is authority today? Like the ferret, we know it has passed but we have never seen it.

Systems no longer stand on a firm hierarchical authority. Even if the ordinary soldier still has to stick to the rules (which are much looser than they used to be), this is seldom because his sergeant yells at him. This makes a great difference in human relations and in the way the system works. The traditional image of hierarchy, a construction of arches and pillars resting upon one another, has become totally inadequate. What we have now is much more like a beehive, where everyone depends on everyone else and controls everyone else at the same time, where nobody commands but everyone obeys.

Some may say that I am exaggerating because there are still people who make decisions that affect the lives of thousands of others. In fact I am exaggerating a little because I want to wake up the pundits who have fallen asleep amid their certainties. But I am not exaggerating that much. Have you ever studied how big decisions are made? Do you know the restrictions on the people who make them? Do you know how often the decisions are nothing but the inescapable result of irresistible pressures brought to bear by the whole system? Do you know what diplomacy, what foresight, what tactical sense an executive must have to succeed just occasionally in making people accept an idea that he feels is important and to make it a reality?

Individual freedom of choice is linked to the extraordinary increase in relationships and interactions between people. But at the same time it is the principal source of the tensions that are eroding traditional authority. Freedom of choice, upon close inspection, naturally leads to the reversal of relations of authority because as soon as a subordinate has reasonable alternatives, he is less dependent upon his superior. Let us look at what happens. Every superior has to take into account the fact that the answers that his subordinates give to his orders will determine his own effectiveness in his relations with his own superiors, his supporters, and the world around him. This means that he depends upon his subordinates to a certain extent. Because they are less dependent on him, because they can easily change their place of employment, their residence, or their jobs, the balance of the relationship is transformed. Of course, superiors still have some weapons and will find ways of directing and stimulating the activity of those under them. But it will be an entirely different game, far different from one in which bosses used to rule a sort of captive audience by means of a solid chain of command.

This is happening everywhere. It is often more pronounced outside of business, in institutions such as education and the church. Throughout the Western world, individual freedom of choice has grown in an extraordinary fashion, without our having realized it. The few remaining traditional barriers cloud our thinking, and we do not think of those that have fallen and the consequences of this. It is not just that men and women can choose their careers, their jobs, their friends, and their spouses without being hampered by the old rules, customs, and conventions. Within each of these relationships, they are freer to the extent that they are no longer bound for life by their initial choice, and because of this they naturally demand much more of them. As soon as it becomes possible to break off a relationship without too much material or emotional cost, the effect of domination is much less easy to maintain.

This reversal is particularly evident among the young, whose relations with adults—parents, teachers, or employers—have changed profoundly. The spread of sexual freedom and the renewed debate over the role of women in society have also speeded up this dynamic transformation. In this context, the myth of traditional authority must crumble. It is true that religious and moral values persist more than is ordinarily thought and that they are gaining in some quarters. But they no longer have a repressive social function. Those who represent or espouse them are listened to but not obeyed. People do need a spiritual experience, but life is too complicated for the faithful to keep on obeying their priests. And as for the clergy themselves, they are too hard to recruit for bishops to risk displeasing them by giving them orders.

In the basic transformation of the relations of authority, all institutions that are founded on them are eventually threatened unless they can discover and put into effect new ways of governing. If the institutions that are engaged in production work comparatively better, this is because they have found it easier to change themselves, devising by trial and error models of governing based on mutual control and the effectiveness of results. Schools and the church, however, have found themselves powerless when the authority of priests or professors has been defied. This raises the central and inescapable problem of the governability of institutions, systems, and whole societies. Sociologists call this the problem of social control. Whether we like it or not, the old ways of doing things are obsolete. Since they do not work, they are being partially replaced by different ones.

Faced with this situation, what are we to do? We have to build, not destroy. It is no longer any use to attack the structures of domination because they are already crumbling and the present disarray of Western humanity is the consequence of this. Now we must create the conditions and means necessary for better management of social organization, to work out other ways of governing ourselves.

Unfortunately discussion of this question usually takes place in the wrong terms because of what I think is a profound mistake in defining what is the matter, one that prevents us from looking at the problem in all its breadth and difficulty. For most intellectuals and politicians and for media of all political persuasions, freedom, security, and the withering away of authority are the solution, not the problem. For others—and they are not only politically on the Right—we have to move backward either partially or entirely to restore values and authority structures based on better aims. Both of these positions are out of date. It is impossible to go backward, whatever the worth of the values of a past civilization of which we can justly be proud. But the fact that we cannot go backward does not mean that we can just knock down the old social structures, believing that this will establish the rule of freedom and justice.

Why? First, let us dismiss one point of view right away, that of all the prophets who today, as always happens in times of uncertainty, are calling for a new egalitarian and libertarian way of organizing society, one without any authority at all. This position is very popular and is held by many in intellectual circles, propounded by those who in other times would have been moderate reformers, such as Ivan Illich. They think that we have too much government, far too many institutions. We have no need of all this apparatus of schools, hospitals, transportation, and police. This point of view responds to the feeling of suffocation that arises with the accumulation of technology and the bureaucratic procedures that make it work.

This is a real problem because it is necessary to simplify, to cut back, to find procedures and arrangements that are different, simpler, and more efficient. But to get better results at a lower price, we must invest in studies, experiments, and supervision. Paradoxically, the simpler and more efficient the result, the more we need a complex institutional framework.

The simplest act of everyday life, such as flipping a switch to turn on a light, requires the development of an enormous and complex structure to produce and distribute electricity. We already know how difficult planning for this is. It also requires the installation of the entire electric system by technicians. In the same way, freedom in human relations and the simplicity of our acts in this area require more and more costly, long, and complex efforts. For example, for students to learn without undue difficulty and to escape the regimentation of the past, their studies must be based on an immense effort of research, and the sequence of their learning must be programmed after analysis and experimentation. And a staff organized more freely, one that is necessarily complex, has to follow and support them so that they can use the course material with ease. The French school system of today seems stupidly restrictive and its programs difficult. This is not because it is too modern but because it is desperately backward, as much in its system of teacher training as in its internal organization. In fact, in these two areas it has hardly changed in a hundred years.

People are not made freer by getting rid of organization but by developing it. Serious consideration of the problem leads us to give priority to the problem of institutions. We have to create the conditions where the social fabric can continually extend and renew itself. For that, we need rules that allow trust, protection, and the regulation of conflicts, as well as of cooperation. If it is not intelligently managed, the social fabric tends to unravel. Management does not necessarily mean authority, but it always requires voluntary action and conscious involvement.

Leftist intellectuals and politicians of the Left as well are no more advanced on this point than those on the Right. They deny the very existence of the problem, and the very policy that a government of the Left would undertake would inevitably make it much worse. Workers' control of industry is not the answer either, because it too would make things worse.

Undergoing a Crisis of Uncertainty, Faced with the Complexity of a System We No Longer Can Control, We Are Panicking

To understand our difficulties, the upheaval we are experiencing, we have to take an active approach and not one of recrimination. The real question is not whether to accept or reject the scandals, injustices, mistakes, and stupidity of our society. What we must do is agree on our priorities and find the strength and capacity to take action to address them.

What is most striking throughout our society is the extraordinary overload of supervisory and managing agencies and the impotence of overworked officials, all of whom are incapable of getting anything done. Everywhere in our society the number of people participating in any given decision has increased enormously, as has the number of points of view that must be taken into account. To accomplish anything, a great number of people, representatives of different groups and different institutions, has to be consulted. The mechanisms of consultation are often cumbersome and slowed down by formal organization. But the problem is not, at bottom, an administrative one. If the possible reactions of the various groups and classes of people involved in a project are not taken into account, it is exposed to dangerous opposition that may cause its failure. Because of this, it may be that the number of steps required to start a new program, each with burdens and risks, has become so great that the original point is lost.

The superiority of democracies is traditionally attributed to their greater openness. An open system is richer, and more efficient because it is more rich, than a closed system, which is poorer because it has so few social contacts inside and outside itself. But it is often forgotten that our system has to be able to maintain a minimum level of regulation. If it cannot, it is threatened with entropy, which means deterioration, and which is a general tendency of all systems. There must be a constant effort of institutional creativity to provide the procedures necessary for its growth. If we look at history from this perspective, it is clear that Western democracies, particularly in Europe, have never been entirely open societies. Their workings have been strengthened by a subtle filtering out of participants and demands that allowed an elite the time and secrecy to act. Today's overload, confusion, and impotence are due to the fact that this model of government at arm's length, without communication, is no longer viable, and we have no other system to replace it.

This is not just a French problem. The complexity of problems has enormously increased, and the means of coping with them has declined in the United States, France, and Japan, whether in developing a new supersonic airplane, building a new airport, or building an urban transport system. After they are finished, nobody really knows how the initial decision was made, who is responsible, and why the big decisions were made the way they were.

The fact that the decisions about the Concorde airplane were very poorly made and that none of the desired results were achieved should not make us forget that the Americans failed with their competitive version, the Supersonic Transport, and that at the time American companies had to lay off thousands of employees. The construction of the Charles de Gaulle-Roissy airport can be criticized from many points of view, but it is a success compared to that of the new Tokyo airport at Narita, which has been paralyzed for three years by the opposition of environmentalists. As for the English, they have proven incapable of building a new airport for London. Looking at the problems of urban transportation, the decisions regarding the Regional Express System are a striking example of confusion and irresponsibility, compared to our Metro that dates back to the beginning of the century. It was undertaken on the basis of grossly mistaken estimates of the actual costs, of the social benefits, and even of the traffic and revenue. But the Californians have gone far beyond us in absurdity. The intercity train of San Francisco, BART, is truly a work of art in this regard. The experts advised against the project on two occasions and it was rejected by a referendum, but it was finally approved after twelve years of bitter controversy, thanks to an unholy alliance of environmentalists and businessmen who waged a tremendous advertising campaign. The job of managing it was given to the man who had run this campaign and who was the only person who could cope with its consequences. But it created a financial bottomless pit and turned out to be technically disastrous. For more than a year, the BART was not able to function more than a few hours per day. At present its operating costs are so high that they are a heavy burden on the municipal budgets involved. And the nearby towns, which had been counted on to enlarge the system, have refused to join it.

Technological progress and the increasing refinement of computing methods have not helped matters. The decision-making system that existed in 1900 for these purposes today appears to have been excellent; discussion was clear and open, predictions were precise, and budgets were balanced. This situation changed because of the increasing centralization of decision making, which gets more confused as it gets more centralized. But it is also because of the necessity of reckoning with a much larger number of pressures and participants. This can be called the "Tower of Babel effect."

The myth of the Tower of Babel explains the confusion of people who are faced with a complex world that they have created and that has overwhelmed them. As soon as people stop understanding each other, the mutual incomprehension of different languages begins. Each person is so specialized that he loses sight of the common task. The fact that mass projects confronted this problem thousands of years ago ought to reassure us about our ability to overcome it. Such predicaments are particularly dramatic in areas concerning the private lives of citizens, such as transportation, urban management, health, and education.[3] They are the direct consequences of technological and scientific progress, of the increase in interaction and communication, along with a growth in freedom of access for individuals and groups.

Another trend has to be recognized. It is one that speeds up and strengthens the impact of all these factors, the inevitable discovery of the environment in the widest sense of this vague term, and is in fact the discovery of the limits of human irresponsibility. A decision is easier when its side effects are negligible or when they can be passed off on the social or natural surroundings. The entire economic development of the nineteenth and early twentieth centuries was accomplished at the expense of the environment, which bore the brunt of the mistakes that were made. But because we can no longer afford to make these mistakes, because it is harder and harder (if not impossible) to take the slightest risk, the system loses its flexibility, and every decision becomes a virtually impossible problem.

This change has radically altered the mechanisms of power without our really noticing it, and we have entered a paradoxical turn of events. In the past it seemed important to demand responsibility to be able to act, but today the rules of the game make it better not to extend one's area of authority in order to keep from being too vulnerable. This is clear in the case of the modern state. Its power long depended on the number of decisions it could make, but today the more responsibilities the modern state takes on, the more powerless it is. Its great weakness lies in its sensitivity to the most shameless sorts of blackmail used today by even highly respectable groups. All other institutions are, perhaps to a lesser extent, in the same situation. But it would be a fatal mistake to add to the prerogatives and responsibilities of the state in order to make it act more efficiently and control what we do not control. This is not a question of being for or against the principle of the state but a diagnosis of what is really going on.

We have to think about our social system to act with knowledge of the facts, which means we have to go against the majority of people. There are decisive moments when the greatest risk lies in following the easy way of what seems to be general agreement. Contrary to what is commonly believed, we need fewer rules, not more, in order to make our society work. To govern, we need less formal authority rather than more. If we go with the herd and impose more control and supervision without reforming the very means of controlling the system, we will increase its confusion and complexity even more, and we will push it to the point where it will crumble and fall apart. Political and social relationships are already too structured, and politicians and administrators instinctively play on this complexity. For them, it is easier and more effective to adapt to this situation and to use the complexity of the world as a shield and a buffer without caring about the consequences. Edgar Faure, a prominent postwar politician, brilliantly summed up this way of acting in a famous statement. When asked, "What do you do when you are faced with a problem that is too difficult?" he replied, "I muddle it up."

Beyond a certain level of complexity, nobody can control results. Credibility, particularly that of the government, declines and decisions seem to come from nowhere. At the same time citizens' feelings of alienation grow along with their selfish demands. The bureaucratic structure can resist this blackmail for a long time, but the moral and political cost is high. Occasionally it gives in, which increases the deterioration of the system.

We cannot resist the Tower of Babel effect by trying to restore traditional social values. We have to experiment with new models for running our institutions and society as a whole. This is more difficult than dreaming of ideal societies, but it is more important.

2
THE REAL FRENCH "DISEASE"

Every Society Must Find Its Own Cultural and Institutional Solution to the Challenge of Freedom

We will not solve our difficulties by blaming Philip the Fair or Napoleon all over again. The growth of personal freedom and the steady increase in the complexity of institutions are common throughout the West. In fact, they are universal. The Western world is more affected by them because it is more economically and socially advanced.

Although the problems are the same, the particular responses to them must be different. The resources and capacities of every society depend on its own cultural and institutional characteristics. A society should invent and experiment with new directions and new models of government on the basis of its own resources and capabilities. The range of possibilities is quite broad. Contrary to those who warn of a new age of barbarism, we are not all becoming the same. Stereotyped answers and models brought in from other countries always fail, even though they sometimes seem to have played a part in starting a process of innovation that is all our own.

Why are these problems so difficult? Why can't we always solve them in the same way? At bottom, the question not only concerns the forms of institutions but power and the relations of power. This is the central bond around which a culture and its institutions develop. Without stretching the analogy too far, I would like to suggest a psychological parallel to make my point.

What people learn in forming their personalities through relations with their parents is a pattern for interacting with other people, and this is basically a pattern of power relations. In the same way, the characteristics of social systems depend on basic patterns of acting and interacting that are formed and "learned" in the course of history. People can bend them but can never get rid of them completely. Of course, a society cannot renew itself or learn and change the way a person does. The psychoanalytic model is far from satisfactory for individuals and cannot be used at all for a social system. The social equivalent of the Oedipus theory is a causal or determinist reading of history that traces the source of our problems to some primordial curse. Alain Peyrefitte may be right when he denounces France's bureaucratic "disease," but he accomplishes little by railing against the past.[2] The only positive suggestion that can come out of that kind of condemnation is that we cannot possibly convert ourselves to having cultural characteristics that have already lost their usefulness in the societies from which they came in the first place. Besides on this score every Western society can be attacked because each in its own way is poorly adapted to the modern world. The grass, alas, is not always greener on the other side of the fence, even if its color is interesting and we can learn a lot from looking at it.

The patterns of interaction and institutional machinery that we come up against are certainly obstacles. But if we really want to succeed, we must also think of them as resources because we have to work through them to change things.

Our Basic Problem Is to Find How to Reshape the Pattern of Social Control and the Relations of Power

The challenge of freedom cannot be avoided, and we are driven to find the answers. Social change does not necessarily or automati-

cally mean that new social forms will appear. People must innovate and experiment to make them appear. They must work
piecemeal on social arrangements, relationships, and the overall
direction of society, for these will allow them to live in the new
world that their past efforts have created.

The problem today is mainly to find out how to respond actively to situations where we have something to learn, and not a
problem of values or ideology. Of course, all change is accompanied by the development and renewal of values. But we cannot bring about change by simply calling for new values, still less
by invoking old ones. Neither praise of the past nor the promise
of a sunny tomorrow is anything but the purest rhetoric. In any
case, we have no control over how the basic values of society, the
only values that matter, change. This makes it impossible to apply
psychological or psychoanalytic models to real social problems.
To resolve the Oedipus complex of fifty million Frenchmen is as
crazy as trying to have fifty million people live as if they were all
inhabiting a single wilderness.

Moreover, changing society is not a political or institutional
task in the usual sense of these terms. No constitutional or social
formula can resolve our problems for us. Reforms in education,
finance, or employment can be tools in a strategy of change, but
they have no value in and of themselves. This is even more true
of revolutionary change, whose blind and destructive effects on
the whole are a backward step.

We must give up all those technocratic patterns of thought that
start from highly sketchy analyses and lead to the imposition of
arbitrary guidelines on resentful citizens. We must deal with the
relations of power, a problem that simultaneously affects the
deepest and most hidden parts of our personalities—our relationships with others—and the most long-range direction of our social system. People of the New Left are correct when they repeat
that we are up against the problem of power, even though they

are still prisoners of the illusions generated by the May 1968 uprising. The fact is that the French, like all other Westerners, will no longer tolerate relationships in which they are dependent. What bothers them the most is being excluded, being kept in a state of subordination. Studies of social trends and surveys by many different organizations show that the need for personal freedom and independence is the most sensitive of human relations today. The most powerful generator of social action is no longer material inequality but the feeling of humiliation.

But those on the Left are mistaken in their answers to this basic need. They start from a totally superficial analysis that sees power and its appropriation by a particular social group as the source of evil. From there they go on to chase that will-o'-the wisp, the withering away of power itself. They are searching for a utopian society ruled by virtue, a search that has reappeared regularly throughout the history of Christianity, from mendicant orders to the Moravian and Anabaptist friars. Also they try to explain a problem that is widespread on the basis of a few social groupings. However much the leftists try, they can only wind up making worse the constraints that oppress people. Even with workers' control of industry, when domination is removed from the more obvious relationships, it reappears in intolerable, unacknowledged ways. The widely discussed experiment in self-management by the workers at the Lip Watch factory at Besançon in the early 1970s does not contradict this obvious sociological truth. On the other hand, replacing one elite with another does nothing to change the relations of power. In fact, it tends to make them stronger because the new elite has not been able to learn the tact of the one it replaced. Finally, it is fruitless to propose, as do the theoreticians of democratic socialism, steps and strategies to lead us from the bourgeois state to direct democracy without falling victim to authoritarian socialism because this would guarantee the worst possible results. The vicious circle of resistance and control is the very basis of bureaucracy.

In fact the Left, even those who advocate workers' control of industry, avoid the universality of the problem of power, independent of capitalism or the state or the market. Although they talk a lot about the problem of power, they really diminish its importance because they cannot admit that the problem resides primarily in our own nature. This is why they are incapable of taking on the responsibility of learning how to work out new patterns for action on behalf of society. Of course, it is always easy to criticize the establishment of today because it tends to deny the very existence of the problem. In France, as in Europe more generally, the establishment tries only to cope with social pressures by means of reassuring recipes and half-baked compromises such as the various proposals for participation, all of which are impractical. Even when they have some experience with unionism, the partisans of workers' management, as in the case of the French Democratic Federation of Labor, are just as much under the spell of technocratic cure-alls as is the Right.

Above all we must ask why, in spite of a freer and more open society, the French feel more humiliated than ever before. The answer is that this is so because they are free and because the system, which has not changed, is all the more oppressive because of that. And if the French have not yet succeeded in working out a new system, that is because they are afraid to. In one sense, they are right to be afraid because what is involved is the destruction of an ancient pattern of social relations. What we really need to do is to build rather than destroy. We will make progress only if we work out new ways of acting that guarantee as little social control as is necessary for a society to ensure that people's behavior is both free and compatible with the needs of others.

*Our Greatest Difficulty Can be Traced to Our Instinctive Tendency
Toward the Monopoly of Power*

Power in itself is not evil; what is evil is its relations and the
structure of the system that maintains them. I would sum up the
situation in France in the following way. At all levels of society
the French, once they gain entry to an influential group, instinctively try to keep other people out. What is more, they continue
to maintain a pattern of government that is based on social distance, secretiveness, and closed lines of communication. This is
what can be called the monopoly of power: everyone has a private preserve. This tendency is easy to point out in small groups
and institutions but is more pervasive than that and shows up
even in temporary social relationships.

Unfortunately any discussion of power usually raises the
problem of legitimacy: what right has one person to give orders
to another? But what is often forgotten is that the most important
problem in human relations is not the origin of the elite but its
degree of openness and the kind of government it exercises. If the
elite is closed and monopolizes power, if it governs people at a
distance and in secret, it does no good to recruit the elite from
among workers and impose a more egalitarian system. Then the
feeling of humiliation will be even stronger. One need only read
the accounts of dissidents from Eastern Europe to understand the
frustration and bitterness aroused by an elite made up of people
from the working class.

Today France essentially is suffering from the way its ruling
circles operate, which keeps it from overcoming technical, administrative, and political stalemates. Our system of public administration is at the heart of these stalemates. In particular, the
power elite of our state is at the same time the cornerstone of the
social hierarchy, including that of business and prestigious pro-

fessions, and also is the model for other areas of activity. This system maintains a pattern of noncommunication at the top of the pyramid that shows up from the top to the bottom of the social ladder. Subordinates cannot gain access to the circles above them, but they can keep their superiors from exercising their power, and they use this paralyzing weapon all they can. This in turn leads those in power to bear down even harder on the rules and the chain of command, and the more they do this, the poorer the results.

Contrary to both conventional wisdom and in contrast to the general growth of personal freedom, the paralyzing weight of bureaucracy has increased enormously over the last thirty years. Some government organizations have pushed this stratified structure to the point where it is totally impervious to direct human relations. This is also frequently the case with businesses. Some of them are just as closed and elitist as the government bureaucracy, and their management is monopolized by castes of professional technicians and the clans of high society. But compared to traditional professions and government bureaucracy, businesses on the whole are shaped by the pressures of their environment. Competition and the need to get results require some openness.

Universities, on the other hand, often are deeply caught up in the passion for the monopoly of power. Each is a closed and protected world of jealous castes, closed off within its own territory. They try to offset their elitism with a bogus populism, but this does not make them any less elitist. The realms of technological know-how, culture, and the media are also driven by a pervasive obsession to monopolize power. Despite a lot of little palace revolutions that have allowed them to adapt somewhat, the real game is still for a person or group to gain and keep some territory. A journalist, like a technological expert, above all looks to make himself a bailiwick where he cannot be contradicted. By controlling both his sources and his public and by manipulating his relations with them to his own advantage, he can exercise a real influence. The only way to increase the quality of technical, political, and cultural debates is real intellectual competition. But France is not ready for this yet.

The political and economic establishments have long practiced the monopoly of power to protect their position, but they can now see that it is being used against them. It would be wrong to welcome this reversal too readily because it is much more important to change the rules of the game than to make the winner into a loser.

French society has changed a great deal and on many levels is in full ferment. But every individual effort, every innovation, stops short. The obstacle is our overall social organization. In politics, economics, and organizations and institutions of all kinds, our system relies on very simple and powerful modes of operation: the fragmentation of groups, statuses, and procedures and the maintenance of social and professional barriers. These procedures impede free communication and allow authority to be wielded secretly at the top, keeping people at arms' length. This power structure was stronger in the past because people were not so aware of it, but it is now being questioned. There are more and more ways of making demands and exerting pressure, and uncoordinated procedures and positions of power are poor replacements for the barriers that have fallen. Although the system is in constant crisis, it continues to work, perhaps because we have failed to build another one to replace it.

The Aggravation of Dysfunctions

The present state of affairs is particularly difficult. It seems to me to suffer from an aggravation of what sociologists call dysfunction, or vicious circles of noncommunication, inefficiency, and disappointment. The low morale of officials and the fashionability of utopias and political illusions are the reflections of this. But it goes deeper and leads to a worse social stalemate.

Our enthusiasm for regulations, our obsession with control of government bureaucracy and all other legitimate but powerless authorities, have gone as far as they can. For thirty years, flow-charts and organizational scales have proliferated. Regulations, some of them recent, have taken the system to such a point that it is in a straightjacket. Every office has made itself into an independent "corps," controlling the entry and promotion of its members. The protective system, for example, that was legally given to the upper levels of the Office of Bridges and Highways, was gradually extended over the last thirty years to eleven successive hierarchical categories, each with its own special status.[3] The social security system similarly provides for no fewer than nineteen different categories of people. In some sectors of administration, innovation has become impossible, and it is harder and harder to see what has to be done. Universities and research institutions are particularly affected by this sickness. The resulting demoralization leads to more demands for protection and, hence, for control.

The complexity of the problems posed by the environment leads to yet more regulation, and the more detailed it is, the more inadequate it is. This leads to fascinating cases of bureaucratic insanity. But efforts at reform can alleviate their effects only temporarily. It seems comical that the decision to construct a high school takes eighteen months and must go through twenty-five stages. This is the result of demands for consultation, conformity to the rules, equal treatment, and various other procedures that are passionately demanded by the very people who later will loudly criticize the slowness of the process. Here is another example. A totally incompetent researcher who has a degree earns 1,000 dollars per month. His work is done by a superbly competent and efficient research assistant who earns only 500 dollars per month because she has no degree. She might be urged by helpful superiors to get the degree except that then she would most probably be transferred to another job, where all expertise she has gained would be useless.

As authority disappears, rules take its place. But the problem is not so much the restrictive aspect of rules as their inescapable complexity. When a person in power decides on the spot what to do about a problem that he understands, he himself can reconcile all the conflicting requirements. But when a decision is made impersonally, the choice arrived at arouses necessarily incompatible demands because many of them correspond to very different cases. And when certain aspects of the particular case cannot be taken into account because no rule covers them, the final decision cannot escape being seen as absurd or out of touch with the needs and wants of the people involved. The bureaucratic alienation that has come about in a world that has modernized too rapidly is due to the pattern described above. It is not due to the characteristics of the technostructure described by René-Victor Pilhes, brilliant though these may be.[4]

At the beginning of the 1970s, the restrictions required by the rules of the promotions schedule in an organization as important as the state telephone administration were so extreme that in most cases there was only a single person who could fill a vacant position according to the rules. So it was impossible to match the problems of operations with the personal qualities (human as well as technical) of the technicians, officials, and engineers involved. This was proven by computer simulation.

I went through some negotiations at the University at Nanterre in 1967 that were totally absurd and that had a decisive role in the radicalization of the sociology students there. The students had called a strike to protest the injustices of the application of the Fouchet educational reform. I was able to find out that there were only forty students directly affected, one of whom was Daniel Cohn-Bendit. After desperate appeals, I managed to get the dean to take care of these cases himself, after consulting a committee composed equally of students and professors. When school began again in January, we found that the Minister of Education could not approve any exception to the rule. This is the point at which most of the students started to lean toward the far Left.

If the insanity of the regulations is indeed insanity, it is so primarily because it defeats itself. Everyone complains of bureaucracy, administration, and officialdom. But how do we react to any problem that comes about as a result of the maladaptation of the administrative apparatus? With a few more rules, with more prohibitions, with a deluge of guidelines. This reaction is as true of the Left as of the Right. Even the ecologists do the same thing. They, too, spout bureaucratic prescriptions such as, "All you have to do is . . ." They do not take the trouble to think about the natural regulations we could depend on in order to restore the balance of our environment. They can see nature as a system but are as yet unable to see people this way.

It is even stranger to find that the same gentlemen who declared that they were fed up with the restrictions of organized society in 1968, with the abuses of rules and the self-satisfaction of the technocrats, were happy to accept the common program of the Left, a whole new wave of restrictive rules and plans. Of course, they consoled themselves that they had to organize against organization, that workers' management of industry had to be planned. But how could they really believe that in order to fight against the abuses of the monopolistic state and the financial elite that they attacked, the best thing to do would be to pull everything together into a structure that was necessarily more monopolistic than ever? This is the clearest possible example of the sort of pathological reaction that has kept us from breaking out of the stranglehold of bureaucracy.

There is another pathology underneath the insanity of regulations, the craze for special distinctions and privileges. On the surface, France is a passionately egalitarian society, where the elimination of inequality and injustices is a primary ideal. In fact, ours is a stratified society that generally has evolved in the opposite direction—toward greater rigidity rather than less. It is a society whose citizens are passionately attached to the distinctions and privileges that divide them. All of the virtuous logic of the French Democratic Federation of Labor, for instance, is based on a faulty analysis. The bosses do not make inequality; it is the very working of the system that does, and everyone has a part in it. The idea of reducing inequalities of status and income runs into the resistance of everyone who has some privilege, particularly the lesser ones. It is significant that the only successful attempts to reduce the moral and material effect of social inequality have been made in private companies. And they are alone in setting up collaborative work teams as well. Even in Sweden, it is the owners of private businesses that are in favor of these experiments, while the unions are rather lukewarm.

The passion for privilege has reached its high point in the government bureaucracy. For the last twenty or thirty years, professionalism has gradually diffused throughout the hierarchy. Every class of officials strives jealously to make its entrance examinations more difficult, to prevent any admissions that are against the rules, any promotion that is not entirely in order. Their essential strategy is to restrict access and to seize new domains. Supervisors have a monopoly just like that of the engineers of the Office of Bridges and Highways. So the stenographer will never become a secretary. The employee can serve the function of administrative secretary for ten years but never get into the upper caste. He himself would indignantly refuse "inferiors" any access to his own domain.

Things are almost, but not quite, that bad in the nationalized industries. The French National Railroad Company is a comicbook version of a corporate society, and the personnel circuit of the French Electricity Authority is tightly restrictive. Even more alarming is the diffusion of this model of operation into the private sector, even if the diverse situations and upheavals wrought by change have concealed its effects for a long time. The discontent of officialdom is closely related to this change. French society has more of a problem with its officials than other European societies; we have too many officials who are generally paid too much, and we have allowed this bureaucratic cancer of stratification, privileges, and status to grow. I hasten to point out, though, that any restrictive measure aiming at humiliating or dismembering a class, in this case or in any other, has led to negative results. The liquidation of the land-owning peasantry led to the appearance of Soviet Communist bureaucrats after all. But it is possible to resist the fatal slide, to work with social functions that would naturally have led to the reduction of inequality, without the obstacles that state and businesses set up against them. It is also possible to present broader possibilities to people whom well-directed social change could put at a relative disadvantage.

The Trend Absolutely Must Be Reversed

It is vital to intervene and to reverse a trend that has become pathological. It would be a tragedy to let it get worse, particularly by giving in to the aggravation of the trend that those on the Left have unconsciously planned. Let us not believe that a system can correct itself easily and spontaneously. There are too many contrary examples of decadence and decline. We also have the examples of people's democracies and the Soviet Union, which are totally locked into a ritual of order, hypocrisy, and alienation. At present we are far from these models, but we are very close to the crises that England and Italy are in. It is possible after a while to get used to the ungovernability and the decline that goes with such crises. But beyond a certain point, the social system becomes unable to cope with its own complexity and suffocates. This is when men panic and revert to outdated ways of behavior. Even the English are beginning to act in aggressive and disorderly ways, and tendencies that could be called fascistic are appearing there more and more.

The problem is difficult, for power can neither be suppressed nor nationalized. Power is like the head of the Hydra and grows back more powerful than before when you think you have cut it off. What we must do is to change the patterns of interaction between people to the point where they are more open and free, so that power limits itself rather than some authority imposed from the outside. Considered this way, of course, the problem looks much more complicated, and we will have to take more variables into account. But this very complication will help us to act more according to the facts and to find more practical solutions.

The French are strongly attached to the present bureaucratic order. They demand useless legal protections. They believe that they cannot act unless they are wrapped in their swaddling clothes. They are afraid to question their own limitations. But at the same time they are rebellious, not only in words, which are not very important, but in actions and practice. We are not lacking in resources, not in attempts and experiments in change. The number of splendid successes in changing the most diverse sectors of society is very large. The most large scale of these took place in agriculture, but there are many others, in business, in manufacturing, and even in the area of education. We are too inclined to think in terms of categories and individual cases and to forget real systems in which people live and whose patterns successfully change. One of the cases I have looked at closely is that of Alexis Gourvennec, who has contributed more fundamentally to changing the style of life and the activity of the farmers of Léon than any other administrative and political decision has for any other social group in France. Gourvennec, a very young leader of the rebellious peasants in the early 1960s, became an extraordinary collective entrepreneur in the 1970s and was responsible for making many poor farmers in Northern Brittany into affluent vegetable producers.

A very deep transformation took place a hundred years ago, a good example of successfully managed change that everyone has forgotten. In the space of ten or twenty years, French society succeeded in replacing the Napoleonic model of government, in which the administration was all powerful and even mayors were appointed. It was replaced by a mixed system that was relatively open for the time, and for today as well, in which local leaders could be active in social and economic development. Why should we not be able to bring about the same kind of change today? In some ways, the problem is certainly more difficult, but the resources are available, and they are more than sufficient. A slow preparation has already taken place, too, and it will inevitably lead to results. A period of crisis is inevitable, but it will be rich in opportunities.

Let us sum up the main parts of our predicament. We request, demand, and require more and more intervention by those in authority. Even if these demands are exaggerated, it is natural that we make them because we cannot control the increasing complexity of our social relations without group cooperation. But our present understanding of social control leads us to give responsibility to the state, whose only available methods are rule-making and hierarchical control. This leads to a vicious circle because these are the things that we resist more and more violently. Breaking out of this circle is even harder because the margins within which we can innovate are limited by the atmosphere of crisis that has arisen in the midst of economic and social instability. All social management is made extremely difficult by inflation and unemployment on the one hand and social tensions on the other. Caught up in this vicious circle, the French, like most other Europeans, give priority to short-term over long-term considerations. We are wearing ourselves out trying to make an inefficient superstructure work because it is still the only pattern of action that we think we can trust at difficult times. Because we believe that we can take no risks, we cannot work out the means and modes we need to run things otherwise.

So we have to solve a complex strategic problem, doing two contradictory things at the same time. We must be cautious in investing our material and human resources under difficult circumstances, but we have to use them quickly and certainly with a hard-headed understanding of the possibilities and the risks. To do this, we have to learn to think realistically in terms of the features of the system we already have, for they have much more to offer than a simple look might show.

3
FOR A STRATEGY OF CHANGE

Social Change Should Not Be Undertaken for the Fun of It

We are forced to innovate by the irresistible pressure of complexity, and we cannot use our increasingly outmoded patterns of organization and government. Whether we like it or not, change has become a crucial problem for modern society.

People talk a lot about change. In the last few years, it has become a catchword of social and, recently, of political thought. But people use it in ritual fashion, without its real meaning. At the risk of belaboring the obvious, I think it is important to emphasize that the world, society, and we ourselves are changing all the time without any direction. This type of change results from the innumerable adjustments that go on within human social systems. But this first type of change leads to a general deterioration if we remain inactive. People must consciously be involved in correcting, redirecting, and reorganizing social change. When I speak of the necessity of change, I mean this second, active type rather than the first. There is no need to oppose or glorify social change either, because our crowing does not cause the sun to rise any more than our complaining keeps it from setting.

From this point of view, a first principle seems absolutely fundamental: social change should not be undertaken for the fun of it. We do not alter things simply because we have a new idea but because we have to. And if we do look for a new idea, it is because we have no choice. No idea of what is good is enough to justify action, and all by itself it will turn into something crazy.

Whether it aims to establish the kingdom of God on earth or to go along with what is fashionable, social change is much too serious a prospect to be based on some ideal plan. We change because it is logical to change, because life is change, and because unless we change we suffocate. On a deeper level, we change to stay alive. Organisms that do not change become weak. Systems that are not regenerated become so complicated that no one can manage them.

Any attempt to change society is a serious step that requires intimate understanding of the details of the situation and how they are changing, as well as a judicious appraisal of the possible risks and consequences. The fact that a plan may look good or that it has a good chance of being supported by most citizens, is by no means enough. If I sound cautious, it is not because I am a conservative who is fond of social hierarchy and disturbed by the consequences of too much democracy. On the contrary, I insist so much on the precautions necessary for serious results because I think that conscious and voluntary change are the necessary touchstone of democracy's growth.

The rhetoric of change has both absurd and dangerous effects. From reading what revolutionaries, and even some moderates, write, it would seem that their implicit strategy boils down to the following plan: destroy and then rebuild. Destruction fascinates them. They dream of capturing fortresses and tearing down prisons. The past must be wiped away, leaving a blank slate. These are the strategies of barbarism, totally inappropriate for the infinitely delicate stuff of mankind. Deep down both revolutionaries and technocrats share this way of thinking, which is based on extortion and repression. Oddly enough, in our complex societies the thinkers who are supposed to be the most sophisticated about social change—including the various forms of Marxism in even its most enlightened version—have remained or reverted to the scorched-earth method. Burn, burn, they say, for out of the ashes life will finally grow the way we want it to. But in fact life consists of our collective ways of acting, our storehouse of skills, our abilities to interact in organized ways. They are not inexhaustible, like virgin forest, and all destruction has its price, which is long in the paying.

Because they are the only way to achieve successful change, the ideas of slow growth and the freeing of potential must be defended against this barbaric scheme. People cannot be transformed by decree, but they can be changed by giving them opportunities, by helping them to develop new abilities and to make use of them. Experiments can be started, helped, made possible, and through them people can learn and change themselves. Conflict in and of itself is not productive, and conflicts that are dominated by the model of destruction and reconstruction are backward and stalemated and have little positive effect. Conflict can become productive only if the combatants get out of their trenches to work out or accept a new way of running things, one that rewards initiative and allows progress to occur.

We Have to Change Our Ways of Thinking

The backwardness and depression of French society today are not due to a lack of material resources. They are the result of intellectual backwardness. We French attach a lot of importance to intellectualism, of course. Our politicians try to present themselves as writers, and our businessmen and doctors play at being philosophers. But all that is show. Faced with the prospect of action, we have become terrible thinkers. There are few other countries that understand as poorly as we how important it is to invest in human abilities, relations, institutions, and patterns of organization.

The real problem lies in how we think. In France, strategy is thought of in military terms, like the principles of Clausewitz, for taking things apart, and in terms of master planning for rebuilding them. Both ways of thinking are entirely inappropriate for delicate human institutions. Destroying the enemy makes sense for soldiers but is senseless in terms of society. How many more times are we going to make sacrifices to this Leninist romanticism? It is really nothing but the thinking of a Prussian general. To make war on the old society is to lose the battle before it has begun. It is not possible to isolate the exploiters, the bad guys, so that they can be liquidated. In medicine, to amputate from a living body is a crude way of curing a patient and can be used only when there is nothing else to be done. For human society, evil does not lie in people or in classes but is part and parcel of the system and its workings.

But the prevalent model for rebuilding is more dangerous because it is more widespread. Building plans for social change means acting as if human beings were inert matter, as if people were not going to react to the goals and limitations imposed upon them. Because the goals are good ones, so the thinking goes, because they are democratic, everyone should accept them. The bulldozing revolutionary dreams of moving battalions, blowing up prison cells, taking the citadels of capitalism by storm. But the technocrat says to the poor politician who is snarled up in his own promises, give me good goals and I will give you sound strategies. Both ways of thinking have in common the simple rational model in which the ends must be more important than the means.

Neither the revolutionary nor the technocrat will accept the basic fact that in social development, the resources are so limited and poor that the means take priority over the ends. There is nothing wrong with this from a moral point of view—quite the contrary, because people themselves are the means. It would be wrong to subordinate people to the objectives that have been set up for them. Glib phrases such as "democratic planning" or "the people as a whole" are nothing but tricks in a con game.

On the other hand, it is not enough to avoid the twin pitfalls of technocracy and revolution by simply giving emphasis to the means used. Our whole idea of strategy has to be changed.

For a Strategy of Investment

Strategic thinking comes out of the experience of war. It is sad that people should have to learn to think as a group through warfare, but all conscious and rational action involves strategy. By this term I mean the use of means available with the aim of winning a particular exchange, while taking into account the behavior of the various participants. It is seldom recognized that what makes war so fascinating is its simplicity, which gives it a great logical force independent of all the suffering it causes. It is not by accident or because of bloodthirstiness that people often use war in figures of speech. It is because war is simple and clear, and all know who the winner is.

To think logically regarding social matters, first we must change over to a frame of reference that has nothing to do with a struggle between two clearly opposed parties. Making war is more complex than drawing up plans because it has to take into account the degrees of freedom of enemies and ultimately of allies. The model of military strategy, therefore, lets us throw out the simplistic model of the technocrats. But real social change is even more complicated than warfare because in this case the enemy is not outside us. As we have seen, we ourselves are the enemy.

Since we cannot use destruction as a threat against ourselves, why talk of strategy? It makes sense to do so because of the hostility between the innovator and the social system within which he must act. This system is not passive: it reacts, and this is what makes the analogy of warfare useful. Because of its complexity, it will not react like a single, undifferentiated actor, and this is what makes the analogy of warfare of limited use. In fact, the only chance of success an innovator has is to go beyond the arena of warfare and to insinuate his changes into the system in such a way that its internal patterns, and workings will change themselves.

So another model has to take the place of military strategy, a model of investment, one that can and should also be considered strategic. In human relations, investment is not something that can be simply calculated. Investments in buildings or in the means of production have their rules and formulas. In spite of imponderables, even investments in the natural increase of the earth and of livestock have a certain regularity. But investment in human relations means using people's capacity to work out and maintain a pattern of interaction that is both more efficient and more complex. This means working with something that is very unsubstantial and difficult to mobilize. To succeed, not only must everyone be more competent but a model of social relations must be devised that allows this competence to be used.

Immediate changes are required to grab the attention and feelings of the people involved, but they are not very effective. Beyond a certain point, they may even backfire because they may be quickly deformed by the structures to which they are introduced. Success can come only though constant advancement, and for this there is no way besides investment. The analogy I am making with economics is not a superficial one. It seems expensive to create new productive facilities by means of investment, but once created, they produce results that change the mechanisms and even the very nature of production. No change in the organization of social life, of human relations, and of decision-making systems can take place without setbacks and immense efforts. These efforts are even more burdensome than is commonly thought but are now both indispensable and more and more profitable.

A strategy of change, therefore, is a strategy of investment, based on a reasoned understanding of the foe (who will be working against change) as well as of friends (who will benefit from it). To say that we ourselves are the enemy implies that in this case friend and foe are one and the same. In other words, in contrast to the strategy of warfare, the strategy of change does not aim to destroy the enemy but to make him into an ally. This takes time, and any action for change has to be understood less as pressure on the enemy than as investment in helping him to renew himself. For this, three main priorities must be pointed out: investment in knowledge, investment in people, and investment in experiments.

Investment in knowledge is necessary for change, although it is remarkable that so little importance is attached to it. No investment in industry is ever undertaken without detailed study of the technological and economic facts, and these themselves are based upon a body of scientific knowledge. But most often reforms of human social systems are undertaken simply on principle, with only the most superficial understanding of the facts.

Investment in people is the precondition for action. No change can take place without human efforts, without the involvement of the people who are going to make them. It is too commonly believed that if a change answers a real need, it is enough that those in charge have enough enthusiasm to overcome all obstacles in their way. Unfortunately enthusiasm neither lasts very long, nor is it much of a compensation for incompetence. The problems of a complex society can be solved only by applying the directives of a leader or applying to the letter the principles of a reform. To make change a reality, innovation has to be decentralized, and many more people have to be involved. How can this be accomplished? How can change be set in motion? By investing in the recruitment, training, and development of people.

Investment in experiments, finally, must be considered. There are no changes without risks, without setbacks, and this means that some endeavors will not yield results. The cost of experimentation has to be thought of as part of the cost of change, partly because even failures have a lot to teach us and because investing in experiments is also an investment in knowledge and people.

French Society's Resources for Change

What is most striking is the abundance of resources available for change in French society. Of course, the main problem is that they are not available for just any change. Many people are competent and have ideas and want to be involved in changing things, but everyone wants something different. The notions of willingness and motivation are not very clear, though, whereas facts and actions need to be reckoned with. And what do we see on this level? Despite appearances, French society is not at all inert and passive. People are not content with just getting by. They are innovating and bringing about all sorts of changes. Many of these answer to the same fundamental need to cope: simplifying, making shorter paths between experience and decision making, finding new ways to manage things that have become too complicated, and setting up relations of authority that allow people to take on responsibilities.

Alexis Gourvennec, a small-scale farmer from Léon in Brittany, innovated when he organized his fellow peasants not in favor of price supports but to work out simple market structures that made it possible to take control of a system that was anarchic, complex, and inefficient. Jean Paquet, a baker from Clermont-

Ferrand, innovated when he organized all his fellow bakers from Puy de Dôme to find a solution to the marginalization that awaited them. In a few years he succeeded in revitalizing the market. And Evelyn Sullerot's innovation was to create, outside the existing structures, a system for retraining women for the job market, short-circuiting the bureaucratic channels of teaching and job training. She broke the vicious circle in which public action tends to perpetuate the very problems it is supposed to correct. There are many other examples that are just as clear but less well known and thousands that are less clear but show a whole host of useful experiments.

No boss, no unionist, no foreman in a factory or workshop so far has succeeded in solving the puzzle of making a truly autonomous production team work according to the model of the worker's management of industry. Scores of them have seriously tried though, and many officials have tried to escape the bureaucratic straitjacket, without daring to admit it. Past and present experiments have also been tried by executives and organizers in the fields of public health, social services, culture, recreation, and tourism. The vision of French society as a desolate expanse ruled by state offices in Paris or monopoly trusts is one of those half-truths that totally warp the way people think. French society is also a living society, probably as alive today as it was in the best of times in history.

It is still stalemated because the innovations that appear in it seem not to go beyond a certain point and because they often do not last. In our society little streams do not become big rivers because powerful patterns of regulation consistently reject any innovation that is not compatible with the rigid workings of its large-scale, interlocking structures. Like a squirrel in a cage, attempts at innovation continue to make the system work, even though they cannot change the system they are working on. And it is noticeable that a subtle equilibrium tends to come about naturally, one that leads anyone who has accomplished anything to become conservative. Like the English colonel in *The Bridge over the River Kwai*, he is so attached to his creation that to save it he is ready to betray his duty as a combatant. So the problem is not one of not enough resources but of the absence of a point of departure and the resulting inability to make use of resources with the system of government.

The Three Principal Sources of Blockage

The trouble with French society is not so much due to the backwardness of its productive forces as to the fact that its main structures are blocked. To analyze this blockage clearly, it is no use blaming the distribution of power, at the top or between bottom and top. Actually the effects of centralization and domination can persist only because everyone shares in letting this happen. We have command at cross purposes rather than a chain of command, and both superior and subordinate are controlled by considerations other than the power structure. Order is not maintained by pressure from the top but by the pressure of neighbors, competitors, and colleagues. The blockages of French society above all are due to the lack of openness and mobility in the workings of its organizations.

In reality, government takes place over time and according to the rhythm of people's lives. The conservatives of today are the innovators of yesterday. Edouard Herriot, one of the most famous politicians of the French Third Republic, was one of the best examples of this. Remember that while for thirty years he was the symbol of conservatism and universal immobility, he had been thought the most dynamic mayor in France when first elected mayor of Lyon in 1905. In a rigid system where innovation is difficult, the successful innovator profits from his situation, and it seems unwise to him to alter it. He also will tend to block off the resources he himself has opened up. So the problem is not one of resources but the ability to make them available to keep the system open.

Octave Gelinier showed how strong this phenomenon is in the case of middle-sized businesses. He calls it the "Latin model of management". It starts with the rapid development of an organization from the innovative resources of a group of founders. The paralysis of the organization sets in ten or fifteen years later when the innovators have become like feudal lords, dependent on the revenue of a situation they have created. Under these conditions a strategy for change must be aimed at opening up the system. Even more than the substance of reform itself, the strategy should stress spacing out action over time and the necessary rebirth of innovative activity.

The very nature of the blockages leads to another sort of observation: the blockage of the power structure is not as important as it seems. Would it not be more effective to concentrate less on organization charts at the top, as is done so often? It might be more effective to try to reduce the extent to which people are cut off and sealed off from one another by encouraging them to be more mobile in what they do and parts of the system to compete more. The larger structures of society rather than organizations are the real problem. French society's paralyses are not evenly distributed. The same patterns show up again and again in very different activities, and the influence of the same cultural outlines can be found everywhere, but their effect can be extremely varied. Some areas of activity where innovation is easy are much freer, while others are entirely frozen. And above all, there are certain fixed points that determine the structure of the whole system and dictate its capacities. From this perspective, what is striking is that on the one hand there are the compressed and rigid systems that control the points of paralysis that are basic to the whole society. On the other hand there are more complicated and fluid systems that are more competitive, where there are areas in the process of very rapid change. To me, three main systems appear to be binding French society and keeping it stalemated: the educational system, the system of public administration, and the system for recruiting leaders.

Education: Ministers come and go, constantly trying to change the national educational system but the problem with it is not its educational mission but the entire body of people who carry it out. Despite its diversity and the different layers of its personnel, this system is so interdependent that it is impossible to change any part of it without changing the whole. It is so interdependent that it is resistant to overall change, whether from the Left or the Right. It is so rigid that its paralysis leads to considerable paralysis for the rest of the society.

The world of education is totally autonomous, and while it may not run itself in complete freedom, at least it keeps its contacts with the rest of society to a minimum. The only relationship with the outside world that it cannot avoid is negotiations with the Ministry of Finance. The schools are not places where ideas are exchanged or enlightenment takes place; they are closed off in principles and habits. But their importance is no less great; far from it. For the whole of society, the schools maintain a cultural pattern of egalitarianism, of stratification, of the fear of face-to-face encounters, and above all of a competitive style of human relations and the intellectual model that is part of it. And they are protected by extremely powerful political and administrative structures.

It is also significant that the teachers' unions are the most powerful in France and that there is a close relationship between the Left and the world of education. While it is impossible to institute piecemeal reform because the system is too interdependent, its central role in the political and union systems prevents any over-all change.

Public administration: Our entire system for decision making and collective action is dominated by the system of public administration, which is as inflexible as it is interdependent. The world of officialdom is complex and layered and reproduces the same pattern of centralization and stratification in all of its components. The consequences of this are imposed on the rest of society, which has to mold itself to the structure of its bureaucracy rather than the other way around.

The French civil service undoubtedly has changed over the years because it is a living entity. It has gone through crises and even through some reforms. But looked at historically, it seems not only to have tended to grow more and more ponderous but also to become more and more burdensome for society as a whole. It is most directly affected by the challenge of complexity, and the best that can be said for it is that until now it has not responded. In any case, any change in any area will conflict with the blockages that make up the collective decision-making practices that depend directly or indirectly on the administrative system. Readers who are surprised by the severity of my judgments can consult my previous writings or Alain Peyrefitte's *Le mal français.*

The system for recruiting leaders: Our elite system is different, of course. It is not a coherent and regular structure like the administrative or educational systems but a network of informal contacts grafted onto formal organizations. It is closely linked to the characteristics of our decision-making system and its strongest leverage is in public power. But it goes beyond an administration that it helps partially to shape, and it deeply influences the most basic areas of activity in society.

If the educational system can be counted as one of the sins of the French Left or of the sociological group it is linked to, the system of elites is the worst sin of the sociological Right, which has never been liberal in the slightest. It is a tightly closed system that allows a very restricted group of people, because of their privileged access to positions of control and their homogeneity, to benefit from tremendous advantages over competitors. The smallness of the number of people and the style of education they receive encourage mutual acquaintances and build up old-boy networks. In the context of the overall system, this elite, or rather superelite, is indispensable for resolving the serious problems of a fragmented society. But the way it functions is what creates the need for its existence. This is where government by stratification, social distance, hierarchy, and ultimately by secrecy comes from.

There are other sources of blockage in French society, but these systems are what maintains the existence of the mode of selection and style of action of those in power, the present machinery for making decisions, and the cultural pattern that allows members of the society to adapt. They are the framework around which the rest of French society is built. By comparison, all other areas of activity seem to be relatively fluid and changing. It is unwise to put too much faith in appearances, for many blockages are hidden behind such relative anarchy. But the focal points of the society lie in these three blocked systems. One measure of this is that since the liberation from the Germans, the financial sector has been mostly absorbed by the administrative system and almost entirely colonized by the elites.

Considering the business sector or the economy in general, many industries are partially or entirely paralyzed because the influence of the administration on financing is very strong. The elite system has great influence on the selection of executives of big businesses and on the pattern of power relations. And actually the social sector seems more susceptible to explosions rather than innovations. But overall it is still relatively open to new ways of acting, and the economy has developed in the last thirty years, in spite of everything. The same is true of regional affairs, and even French cities have been fundamentally changed, in spite of administrative roadblocks. A whole new way of life has appeared in the countryside and in the cities, without the crises that accompanied this change in Italy. The same is also true in services, recreation, and tourism. In all of these areas, many original experiments and solid innovations can be found that are not like other dead-end reforms.

Finally, it may make sense to think about changes in values and how they can be a source of social renewal. The new aspirations of women and young people are not just political and social demands but a new resource that may complicate social relationships but can be used as a means of change and overcoming blockages.

Transforming Demands into Resources for Change

Society is neither soft clay that a reformer can knead nor a totally hardened structure that must be blown apart with dynamite. It is a whole system in motion, in which a huge mass of energy is at work. The real barrier to social change is the fact that these forces are diffused, or rather that they are channeled in negative or conservative directions. The fact that energy is present does not mean that society will develop all by itself, nor that these energies can necessarily be used in a positive way. In fact, they can be simply translated into demands, which help to keep things as they are. To me, the main strategic problem seems to be how to transform these demands into resources for change.

There is a contradiction between the necessity of breaking with the past and the danger that this entails. It can be overcome only by finding the pressure points of the system, by depending on the capacities of people to behave in new ways, and by channeling investments so that they will develop these capacities. The problem cannot be resolved in an instant, and it can be grasped only if we are patient and bide our time. And it cannot be resolved unless we go beyond the narrow structure of each institution involved. By working with time and space, the strategist of change can avoid a confrontation that would exhaust him.

What should we do in the case of the administrative and educational systems, both of which are too interdependent, cut off, and autonomous to be changed from the outside or the inside? Well, the first thing to do is to be realistic. Confrontation is useless because officials or teachers cannot be changed by decree. A defensive strategy must be adopted, one of not attacking or even threatening fortresses that for the moment cannot be conquered. It is better to use strength, time, and energy on other systems, not to reform sectors in order of theoretical importance but the ones where there is better chance of success. In other words, it is better to create a process of change and to free new, positive forces.

Does this mean that we have to give up on the important systems? And what advice can we give to those who are prisoners in them? Certainly it means we have to agree to act differently: not direct confrontation but long- and middle-term preparation by investing in people and in knowledge. Any moderately reasonable Minister of Education would give up on the guerrilla warfare of reforms. He would devote his energy and means both to force the educational system to understand itself and to absorb this understanding and to train teachers and administrators to use this knowledge to learn new types of relationships.

The reformer, should, however, take action in the murky and poorly integrated area of higher education. His chances of success would be greater there, and he could also call forth human resources there to be used in the attack on primary and secondary education. But even in this case, problems should not be confronted head on. Contrary to short-term logic, we must not reform the universities, which work poorly, and leave alone the elite training schools, which work well.[1] First of all, we must reform that which is working well, the elite training schools, so that we can then work on the university system, which today is impervious to reform. Why? Because in the elite training schools there are forces that can be mobilized immediately, young leaders who can be switched from making demands or demanding confrontations to constructive work. Because the elite training schools are where the administrative, educational, and elite systems intersect and are therefore very sensitive and vulnerable.

The same logic applied to the civil service impels us to give priority to territorial or regional reform. Why? Because at the moment it is impossible to affect the legal status of public service, which is one of the essential points of French political sensibility. And because without a change in this status it is fruitless to undertake constructive action.

Social structures cannot be changed without changing the way people think, and we cannot change the way people think without changing social structures. But it is possible to change the relation between the administrative system and society and so change the conditions that shape both ways of thinking and social structures. How? By transforming the relations between officials and leaders, whose hidden and almost unconscious interaction is what really shapes politics and the civil service. Even though the bureaucracy is protected, it is vulnerable because it is out of date and stifling. It is possible to go beyond it to a new type of interaction, of which the people involved are capable and for which many other forces can be mobilized. It is possible to play off regional elites against the administration or young leaders against the entrenched powers that be.

Naturally it is possible to object that this strategy is difficult, and too risky to take seriously. In the following chapters, I will explain at length what I mean. But I want to say now that if positive change is highly improbable, all social progress is none-theless the consequence of such highly improbable changes. At present what is important is to choose intelligently the sensi-tive points where we can act and the areas open for development where we can push ahead. To start off on the difficult road of re-sponsible social change, we cannot act directly to resolve prob-lems in the way a technocrat or a soldier would. We must choose our area of action, our problem, and our means on the basis of our chances of success. If the problem is insoluble, we must change our area of activity. If there are no means available in any area of action, we must turn to another problem. Society as a whole must be reexamined as a field of resources and problems where, by making one match the other, innovations can be made to appear.

Thus inequality cannot be attacked by restrictions and repres-sion, but conditions can be created to make economic relations move in this direction. What are the resources in this case? The interaction of business and market, the ones that, unfortunately, people too often want to suppress. More equality can be created by using business and the market against bourgeois or rentier thinking than by imposing restrictive salary structures and schedules on all businesses. And there will be no redeployment of industry that generates jobs without investing in services, re-search, and everything that appears to be inefficient, against what appears to be of basic importance. There are many more resources and possibilities for change in sectors that are still open or ready to be opened than in the main sectors, even of high tech-nology industries. After all, the first industrial revolution of the eighteenth century started in weak areas of the economy that were minor and totally unprotected.

It is possible that the same approach could be used to deal with the inescapable and insoluble problem of the demands of women. It is not possible to make conditions for men and women equal in a short period of time, either by equally distributing today's jobs, which would devastate men, or by doubling the number of jobs available, which would require a crushing growth rate and an unbearable weight on currently available economic resources. However, it is possible to provide opportunities for involvement and even for leadership in a whole new frontier for women who want them. The areas that are rapidly changing through the very pressure of evolution are those where women's cultural attributes would make them particularly productive: social services, education, health, the quality of life, and the new high-level services. To those who argue that these areas are second-rate activities, I would answer that they are in the process of becoming first rate. People who are moving up would do well to choose these fields, where the chances of success are much better than in the traditional fields.

4

THE BUREAUCRATIC PHENOMENON

Taking On the Civil Service Is Both Impossible and Essential

The greatest cause of blockage in France is the administrative system. The bureaucratic phenomenon is immense and can be found everywhere. The educational system is a case in point. The schools cannot be changed because they, along with the teachers, are part of a huge state bureaucracy. And the elite system of decision-making, the third main source of blockage, finds support and protection in the civil service.

Any consideration of a strategy for changing French society must take the administrative phenomenon as its starting point. This priority of thought does not necessarily imply a priority of action though. It means that we must think first about what is biggest and most important, but not attack what cannot be changed right away. We are faced with our first paradox in this regard. On the one hand the administrative system oversees all of the possibilities for change in our society, and it is very difficult to get anything done without reforming it, but on the other hand it is almost totally impervious. Everyone wastes time condemning its misdeeds, without having the slightest effect. So inevitably, here is the problem of the instrument to be used for reform: you cannot change the administration by administrative means, and you cannot change officials by making official decrees.

The very immensity of the system makes it both unbearable and impossible to affect. It is everywhere, and it is perfectly co-herent in its workings, not only imposing restrictive rules but also enforcing strong regulations that prohibit any variation from the norm. In most areas of life, it is impossible to innovate without coming into contact with it. An area cannot be substantially changed beyond a certain point without reforming the supervisory administration itself. This means that the administrative system cannot be transformed piecemeal in small steps. It is resilient enough to absorb easily any reforms without really changing its basic machinery, so it has to be taken on in its entirety. But by what means? And does this not mean getting into a vicious circle of constraints?

The only hope of overcoming this contradiction is to think strategically. If the problem is insoluble by this way of thinking, it has to be posed in a different way, or changed. So first let us ask in a more utilitarian fashion why change is necessary, leaving aside the fact that our system is bad. When we have thought about this, we can try to be clearer about what the problem really is. Then the sensitive and vulnerable points of the system, as well as the hidden resources it is harboring, will appear.

Why Do We Have to Act Right Now?

Too often people hesitate between two positions that are both so extreme that they are untenable. One is declaring that the system is bad and that it must be radically changed, and the other is admitting that even though it is bad, it is the product of the French character and that it would be best to keep it as it is. The first position has the advantage of logical consistency but is impractical and leads to nothing but self-righteous talk. The more denunciation there is, the less action. As for the second, just because radical change is impossible does not mean that we should be content to keep things as they are. Perfection may be impossible, but this does not mean that we should not try to do better. It is worth remembering that any system that is not reformed tends to deteriorate as time goes by.

We must act right now because our system already has deteriorated and because the pressures it will be subject to threaten to speed up this deterioration and engulf the whole society in a process of implosion. Our management techniques and modes of regulation are not adapted to the new challenges of growth and change in the social organism. This is one of the natural consequences of the movement toward more complexity and freedom that I have analyzed. I now want to show its palpable and practical aspects in French administration today. I will take two basic examples, urbanization and industrialization.

The Challenge of Urbanization
With regard to urbanization, for a long time France maintained a unique equilibrium that was closely tied to its mode of administrative organization. In contrast to its European neighbors, it had managed to modernize while keeping half its population in rural areas. This equilibrium was destroyed on the morrow of World War II. In twenty or thirty years, the population of France became urban. At present two-thirds live in cities and scarcely 20 percent live in truly rural areas. This exodus, which aroused strong emotions for and against, unquestionably has been the most remarkable aspect of our social life. It happened for better or worse; the cost people paid was doubtless too high.

The civil service was able to manage material changes and more or less to build the necessary framework, ensure investment needs, and oversee change rather than anticipate it. But it has not itself adapted to this change. The French have changed, but not their civil service. It has remained attached to a pattern of management more suited to a rural style of life so it is incapable of understanding, far less coping with, the complexity it is proud of having created.

Any serious analysis of administrative practice shows that the wasteland of French bureaucracy is in the big cities. There citizens are alienated, officials are discontented, and everyone denounces the regime, as in the play *Ubu Roi*. [1] In the country, the residents of villages do not feel alienated at all, and the bureaucracy seems accessible, protective, and close. This is not an illusion. The citizen in the countryside actually does have easier access to the decision-making process in Paris than does anyone living in a big city, and particularly more than anyone actually living in Paris itself. [2]

This is because the French civil service, far from being a bloodless technocracy, used to be based on a foundation of local notables. The village resident and small-town dweller still has easy access to his mayor, who is in constant contact with responsible officials in the area. The mayor and the departmental assemblyman may seem helpless in the face of the all-powerful bureaucracy, and in fact they are as far as attempts at management and development are concerned. But they are far from helpless when it comes to interceding, mediating, and righting wrongs for people. Not only are they listened to; their intervention is actually welcomed and sought out by officials. The responsible officials of the area—tax collector, district engineer, school superintendent—need these contacts and advice to keep in touch with the people they administer to. This relationship is so close that in effect the official is becoming like a local notable, while the local notables themselves have become experts in techniques of administration. [3]

This system has stood up to increasingly severe criticism because it has obvious advantages. It has integrity because mutual oversight greatly reduced corruption. It has humanity because in spite of skepticism, people and their needs and weaknesses are taken into account. It has wisdom because its participants are slow, but they accumulate a great deal of experience.

This rural pattern, which can be praised as one of the successes of the French character, has proven totally maladapted to the world of big cities we have created in the last thirty years. Actually the city, and especially the new city of the suburb, has no notables, or at least no notables who are close to the people. The spectacular climb to power of the mayors of the big cities has been praised, and with good reason. But even if a "big mayor" has contacts in Paris and can gain the favor of the technocrats, it means little to the average person, who has no access to the mayor or to the official with whom the mayor has influence. There is no intermediary.

This maladaptation is also striking when officials themselves are asked to speak. For every alienated citizen, there is a bemused bureaucrat who has lost track of where he is supposed to be going. This demoralization is much more discernible in newly created administrative agencies that have no traditions and no linkages with notables, such as health, construction, environment, and social and cultural affairs. But older and more prestigious administrations are affected by it as well. Officials of the Ministry of Finance, who are by far the most highly respected by the public, are much less comfortable in the city than in the country, contrary to stereotype.[4] And the engineers of the Ministry of Public Works, who are prominent in the countryside, dislike metropolitan areas, where they operate very poorly.[5]

This disequilibrium may not seem very substantial from a distance. The public is used to thinking in simple terms, only blaming people. And those in power, particularly high officials, pay little attention to practicalities. This phenomenon is perceived only by its surface manifestations: irritation against paper-pushing bureaucrats, the bad reputation of technocrats, and centralization in Paris. The response consists of attempts at deconcentration or public relations efforts, which usually only irritate people and complicate things more. However, one of the most pressing needs regarding the quality of our lives is to be able to adapt the administrative and political systems. And the economic, social, and cultural development of the country demands the active existence of an open and effective democratic system rather than grand slogans about participation and self-management.

Industrial Policy
Industrialization was another striking postwar phenomenon. Its problems have not appeared clearly yet but will be dramatic in the very near future. Here again, the support of the centralized state is both pervasive and essential. Until the 1960s we had to deal with what was basically a complex traditional sector, organized around mediating networks of notables. For the individual producer, the problem was one of access. For the civil service, in each industrial branch the problem was the regulation of markets and innovations, as well as organization, which really amounted to restricting competition.

The planning authority sought to turn this system in the direction of greater development. As in the case of the contrasts between administration in country and city, real industrial policy was split between a system of technocratic initiative, inspired by the Ministry of Finance, and a traditional protection system.[6] The opening up of national boundaries has not ended the onerous Malthusian relationship between protectionist officials and factory owners. This system worked as long as European expansion was going on. The technocracy protected very large businesses, which were thought to be the only ones capable of coping with international competition, while the traditional bureaucracy allowed the rest of the industry to hold on. Development could take place without too many conflicts. But the inability of the administration to manage effectively and to work out an industrial policy that was not just following in the wake of international development became more and more obvious as it happened. The fact that the system's financial management was good should not conceal the fact that the choices made were not as logical as people thought they were. Quantity and overall rate of growth were chosen over quality and critical areas for change. Mergers were imposed without enough thought to their suitability and without realizing the enormous difficulty of managing organizations that are too big. Too much faith was put in adding employees, which was supposed to create the "critical mass" thought to be necessary.

This is not the place to discuss the content of the industrial policy, or what passed for one, that was followed. What I want to show is the fatal nature of these poor choices, which were made by men who were highly competent but blinded by the workings of the system. There was no end to the strategic mistakes made over the years. We always chose the worst time to invest in steel production, data processing, telecommunications, or aeronautics, to mention only the areas where the bureaucrats were in control.[7] We seemed never to be able to predict rising curves of development. The success of the Japanese and the Germans has been due to the quality of the expertise they have in market research, industrial management, international resource allocation, and technological forecasting. Our system gives priority to general financial and administrative expertise, both of which tend to stifle precise and empirical specialties while encouraging the humanitarian and Malthusian management of little problems and off-the-cuff improvisation with big ones.

Whatever the most qualified of our experts think, the reform of our system for administering finance has become a question of life or death. It has become pointless to discuss in the abstract the limits of state intervention and the beauties of liberalism. In a society like ours, the state has to be involved, but at the moment it does not seem capable. If we do not change our habits, we will be condemned to act defensively and at the last minute. We can survive only by maintaining the offensive and relying on expertise.

Other Upheavals We Can Expect
The challenge imposed by the new urbanism and the integration of our economy into a world system are not the only upheavals we will have to face. Of the problems that will soon appear, I will cite two that will be particularly crucial for the French administrative system. One is the spread of data processing and modern means of communication and management. The other is the increasingly stronger tendency for activities to be transferred to the service sector, particularly services to business, health services, and social and cultural services.

The computer is still thought of as a sort of deus ex machina that will enable us to manage complex things effortlessly overnight. Of course, this is a snare and a delusion. The success of some sectors, which has been limited in any case, should not deceive us. To succeed and be profitable, data processing requires the kind of clarity that is entirely unknown in the civil service's pattern of action. It leads to the elimination of intermediaries and networks of influence that have developed around and are based on long-standing focal points of communication. Modernizing management with computers is a means of simplifying it, clarifying it, saving time and effort, but it also means making people learn the facts and making every person take responsibility for his own performance. If people are not able to devise new shortcuts and ways of protecting themselves, then the system becomes unworkable.

The movement toward services and sociocultural matters will

bring on another imbalance: the maladaptation of our methods of managing people and of the machinery for making decisions about what has to be done and what problems need to be solved. A growing number of public activities will be devoted to the jobs of management, development, health, communication, the quality of life, social problems, recreation, and culture. What all these jobs have in common is that they deal with fairly complex human relations and imply a certain feedback between the person in authority and the people he is administering. In addition to the role of the old-fashioned official who is also a notable and the expert in new economic and social functions, there is a new role, that of the promoter, the facilitator and organizer of activities. At present it is impossible for such a promoter to survive for long in the world of French public administration. Many of our officials do have the kind of qualities needed, even though their education has not developed them. But the hurdles of qualifying examinations, the way careers are organized, the kinds of rewards and sanctions, and the mode of organizing work and the style of decision making totally paralyze even the most gifted people. In an understandable reflex action, the administration tends to stifle activity that it cannot manage itself. There again, the required development that is relevant for employment problems can take place only if the administrative world is changed.

The sum total of these pressures makes it clear that the equilibrium we have been used to is breaking down. In the next ten or twenty years we are going to enter a period of deep crisis and renewal, which will surely affect the whole society. If we do not realize this, we run the risk of acting too late when the consequences of the breakdown have become unbearable. Then the cost of changing will be immense. Intervening in society right now is not the dream of some technocrat. It means working early enough to enable French society to adapt better.

What Is the Problem in Question?

The changes French society has undergone and the greater changes that probably await call into question the pattern of administration to which we are accustomed. The problem is not one of knowing if it is good or bad in itself but finding out how and why it is maladapted. All societies have had to face these serious transformations, but the general problem is also different in each particular case because what is forced to change includes the means of government and the system of power with which each society regulated its social organism. To adapt and survive, French society will have to find the necessary resources in its own tradition.

What is striking about the French civil service, perhaps even more than its great difficulty in changing, is its inability to see the reality that is threatening it. The contrast between the intellectual quality of individuals and their collective inability to act and to work out a coherent understanding of what is wrong should be a warning to us. Such, for example, is the problem of the consequences of urbanization, which has thrown our social system into turmoil for the last twenty years. The arguments presented in the public debates are theoretical assertions about the principles and conditions for good administration. The ways in which officials, and the people they administer, experience change is never discussed. People responsible do not know, and do not want to know, anything about it.

For more than ten years, one of the important ideas under discussion was the merging of communes. Local democracy and decentralization, it is said, are not possible because of the fragmentation of local government. The number of our communes is so enormous—we have more than all our partners in the Common Market put together—that each one is impotent. They must therefore be grouped together. This reasoning is very logical in its premise but ignores two fundamental facts: our political and administrative system worked well in small communes and poorly in large ones, and the population of little communes is constantly falling (by the mid-1970s, they only included one-fifth of the population). How could French local democracy be revived by merely imposing a brutally rational model on this minority of the population, who are attached to a traditional system that has worked and is still working for them? After learning from its many failures, the government decided to give up the plan for merging the communes. It is interesting to listen to the arguments presented by the minister in charge: the problem was not analyzed, it was simply reversed. These 36,000 communes, which set us apart from the rest of Europe, which made us a nation of little landholders as backward as the time on their bell-tower clocks, suddenly became for him a sign of a richer democracy, which our neighbors were supposed to envy. With 500,000 town councillors, we were supposed to hold the European record for local democarcy, by far. The minister and the members of his cabinet do not seem to realize that four-fifths of these town councillors were serving only one-fifth of the population, and most Frenchmen, from a numerical point of view, are less well provided for than are the Belgians, Germans, or English.

For twenty years, we have desperately sought to reform, organize, democratize, decentralize, without seeing the reality of growing and accompanying deterioration in key areas of administrative activity, Technocratic measures were taken in response to the ensuing problems, which speeded up the centralization that was supposedly being fought. When General de Gaulle finally came out in favor of regionalization in 1968, he immediately added the reform of the Senate to his proposal, which would have meant the elimination of contacts that were essential for small communes to have access to decision makers in Paris.

Despite the very clear evidence on this point given by public opinion polls, it was concluded that the defeat of the referendum meant that the French were against regionalization. In fact, they favored it, but since the kind of regionalization that was being offered meant the dismantling of a system that was satisfactory to an important minority, the French voted to defeat the proposal.

The same administrative distortion and bureaucratic short-sightedness prevented us from working out an industrial policy for twenty years, in spite of all our efforts. We are not stupid, but we have never built the institutional instruments needed to work out a policy. We simply do not have the human means to help us to see reality, to provide the expertise to respond to a fast-moving technical and economic scene that would force us to be practical. We have not even succeeded in formulating the problem correctly. We still keep on believing that it is enough to be intelligent, that knowledge and practice come all by themselves. The problems are entirely different, but we risk botching the computer revolution and the service revolution in the same way, even though we have all the means at hand for doing it right.

What is in question here? It is not the competence of officials, not even their way of thinking. It is the system that they live in. We have to look squarely at this system for a moment without thinking of trying to find out who is at fault. Two basic principles govern the working of French public administration, which make it impervious to reality and to change. These are the principle of stratification, which governs how people are used, and the principle of centralization, which governs how decisions are made. The application of these principles is contrary to many values the French are fond of. Everyone criticizes distance, imperviousness, segregation of different levels, and the blind authoritarianism of an inhuman bureaucracy. But at the same time these principles ensure both equality among people and protection against arbitrary power. They also allow people to avoid conflict, insofar as the lack of power of direct superiors over their subordinates (the consequence of stratification) and the passing on of responsibility to superiors (the consequence of centralization) free officials and, to a lesser extent, those they deal with, from any uncomfortable face-to-face confrontations. While the French reject stupid and oppressive bureaucracy in the name of values, they would love to believe in, at the same time they contribute to its existence by doing and expecting things inspired by other values, which go deeper.

The French administrative system cannot be summed up just in the application of these two principles though. In practice, it shows great tolerance for informal power relations that the very rigidity of the system produces as a matter of course. At first sight the paradox is striking. There is no modern administrative system as rigorous, not to say absolutist, as ours. At the same time, there is no system that is so tolerant of exceptions. "Hard doctrine, soft practice," said Tocqueville. Exceptions, of course, only rarely involve people's rights, and they mainly concern how things are done in practice. They are what allows this huge organism to adapt, because its strictness blinds it to the constant changes of an all-too-living world. In making exceptions, an official does his part and shows—at least to himself—that he is independent, original, an innovator.

What are the practical consequences of this mode of government? To begin with, communication is deeply flawed. The barriers between the levels are also obstacles to communication. Every rank, in its own interest, hoards the experience and knowledge of its members. Those in power cannot be in touch with reality when it goes through the distortions imposed by the successive levels that monopolize information. The data on which they act are false or at least irrelevant. Reality only shines through a prism of bureaucratic logic that distorts it. What is worse, the innovating officials who have played the game of informal power in order to build up a private preserve where they can try new things, who in a way are the only real activists in the system, immobilize and cancel one another out. Moreover, everything that they learn, which could be highly useful for everybody, remains hidden because the innovator has to protect himself, and he can keep his power only by keeping it secret. The system encourages everyone to get as much as he can out of it and to give back as little as possible.

Finally, what is most serious is that respect for real facts is lost. Only administrative facts are left, facts that are worked out by specialists based on a narrow category of knowledge. We have no business-based industrial policy because the machine is unable to find out the relevant facts about real businesses, which are too specific a category to be understood. The relations between the administration and those administered are deteriorating in urban areas, but this is not understood because there is no administrative concept for such a process. This explains the extraordinary difficulty the machine has in adapting. It cannot learn from its experience because it refuses to understand it. It spends its time generalizing and putting together ideas on the basis of irrelevant data. In these conditions, our great reformers dream of brilliant offensives and heroic attacks from their fortresses, with little real chance of success.

What Should Be Changed?

We seem to have come back to where I began with this overgeneralized diagnosis. I criticized the judgments that led to simplistic suggestions like, "All you have to do is . . ." But the natural conclusion of my analysis is to condemn the system, which is not evil in itself but is incapable of adapting. Does this not lead us inevitably to prescribe its radical transformation?

Let us go back to our original discussion of strategy. A good strategy does not consist of pinpointing what is good from the point of view of deciding what is bad but of discovering, through the workings of a system and their consequences, how to put pressure on it so that it will change and learn. You might say, however, that I just asserted that the system was incapable of learning anything. As a matter of fact, I overdid it a little bit to make things simple and clear. Now I will try to go back and discuss more freely, with as few value judgments as possible, the strategies required by the existence of these problems and restrictions.

I think that two steps are necessary to succeed in this. First, think about what has to be learned, how the system should evolve to respond to the problems it faces. Second, identify the resources that can be used for action. "What should the system learn?" is my question, rather than "What should be changed?" as we are accustomed to hearing. And I will answer by discussing the four most sensitive points, as I see them: the adaptation of people and the system to the kinds of tasks that need to be performed, the processes of administrative orientation and action, the use of knowledge and information for working out options, and the style of adaptation to the environment.

The Kinds of Tasks to Be Performed

The nature of administrative tasks has changed a great deal. In particular, it has become more diverse and can be expected to become even more so. Choices were made, in 1945 in particular, that led to standardization of the rules of management, which was totally contrary if not to the needs then at least to the problems that were encountered in the field.

An official finds out the meaning of his function by carrying out his job, and whatever may be said, he is very sensitive to it. The alienation of the bureaucrat, part of the machinery of government, corresponds to that of the citizen manipulated by the organization. Neither is a necessary consequence of rationalization; still less are they the sign of a crisis of civilization. They are the product of a system whose functioning tends to take the human dimension out of a job and the social relations that go with it. To rediscover this essential dimension, official functions have to be thought out again in terms of the human relations they are based on. These relations typically are very diverse and require very different types of independence, support, and rewards, depending on the case. Let us first look at the most traditional functions, which could be called those of law enforcement in the widest possible sense. These are the functions where the application and interpretation of legal norms or impersonal regulations come into play. There are more of these than is commonly believed. They go far beyond the workings of the laws of the state. Many of the tasks assigned to the Ministry of Finance are of this sort. We do not want a government auditor to behave like a businessman or for a tax collector to be paid by commission. We basically want such officials to be just, equitable, and humane. This means that their independence should be guaranteed and that they should be protected from their superiors as much as from the people they deal with. We would be willing to accept not having easy access to them if we knew that this was the price that had to be paid to prohibit all favoritism, pressure, and blackmail. For this sort of role, the system of stratification and centralization is a solution that may have its inconveniences but is not bad. Many jobs more or less have these same characteristics, such as surveillance and control over code compliance regarding job safety, health, and the environment. The boundaries are often hard to define and, depending on choices, a different policy suggests itself; the problem of the police, for instance, should at least partly be dealt with in this way.

While law enforcement functions thus require the protection of officials and impersonal relations, the same is not true for management functions, which demand active relationships with the surrounding world and demand some results. We do not ask that telephones be distributed impartially by an equitable administration but that they be provided to everyone at a reasonable price.[8] We know that this is what happens when telecommunications are well managed. We want its executives to have a businesslike attitude, to know how to invest at the right time, and to know how to innovate. For that to happen, the results that they get have to be known and rewarded. In this instance, the pattern of stratification and centralization is disastrous, being both tempered and paralyzed by informal power relations. Although there are few jobs that point out so clearly the action of a lone manager, there are more than is commonly thought, and they have an appreciable weight in the equilibrium of the overall system. Many others have enough evident potential for action and reward to make it worthwhile to take them out from under the bureaucratic system. For instance, there is no reason why the management of highways and harbors should be handled as a function of law enforcement.

The protective bureaucratic spirit, which is appropriate for the enforcement of laws, is destructive when it comes to many other functions that have nothing to do with management and which are in the process of extremely rapid development, such as technology and activities of promotion and development. The modern state must become involved in some growing activities that cannot develop without state regulation. The state has important economic functions in the areas of research and development, employment, and exports. It would like to have an industrial policy. For all these tasks, it needs many experts, whose relation to the world around them is entirely different from law enforcement or management. The failure of the administration's research staffs should come as no surprise. The State Audit Office was totally wrong to criticize their mistakes.[9] That office is tied up in the logic of law enforcement and is altogether incapable of understanding researchers' problems. More serious than the problems of the research offices, there is a striking absence of experts who are really competent in all of the functions the administration takes on. The only solution is to get a system into operation that is not based on the efficiency of its management or the bureaucratic rule of law but on the standards of excellence of a scientific and technical community that has yet to be created. Such a system naturally implies contracts of limited duration, with salaries and prestige high enough to make up for the resulting lack of security. For decision makers to be free, there must be a regular turnover of experts, who themselves would become much freer because of this.

Other functions, which are entirely different, involve the same sort of standards. These include all the functions of organizing cultural activities, which public officials perform very poorly. Certainly institutions other than the central state, such as towns and regions, could take on social and cultural functions. It is imperative that the content and development of these programs be well planned.

The Management Processes of Administrative Action
The first fact to consider in guiding the course of our administrative system is the nature of its functions, but the processes of control are just as much of a problem. In France the two issues are too easily confused because upper-level French management is guided by a certain idea of control over administrative action that gives priority to executive control as a means of action. Top French administrators, who have the intellect and sometimes the

competence of a prime minister, cannot get anything done without being bogged down in management. And this often happens to the prime minister himself.

I think that one of the most important reforms to carry out is the institutional separation between political control and the regulative functions and operational responsibilities that it involves, whether the latter are those of management proper, of law enforcement, or of cultural organization. It is also one of the most difficult to carry out because in the present system the executive who gets rid of his options for involvement in management leaves himself helpless. So another model of control of public activities is needed, one that is based on intervention by regulation and not on control and decision making. Given our present way of doing things, this is impossible, but it is essential.

The Use of Knowledge and Information for Working Out Options

The greatest paradox of the French administrative system is that is has a truly extraordinary number of able people (not just at the top levels), that intelligence and culture are its basic and highly respected values, but that the system as a social group is incapable of developing, far less of using, the knowledge that it needs. Its information system is inadequate, and it is not even capable of realizing this.

The transformation that has to take place is simple in theory but involves insuperable difficulties from a narrow sociological point of view. What is at issue is the basic shape of people's values and social relations. It is not enough to breed a new race of experts. A whole new intellectual freedom has to be created, and the hierarchy that is now stifling it has to be opened up. Institutional innovations and a long-term social learning process can and will allow this to happen. But at issue is opening up the elites, and institutions other than the public administration system are involved.

The Mode of Adaptation to the Surrounding World
Public functions almost always involve some relation with the surrounding world, which involves the whole society and its political choices. The French style of public administration is based on a deep division between the administrative apparatus and the society. This separation is more or less acceptable when it comes to the enforcement of laws, as we have seen. But for making choices in the distribution of resources, investment, and management, the old barriers must be torn down and be replaced with new and more dynamic systems of action. The present systems are based on a lack of communication, which is what gives such great power to their few legitimate representatives, such as notables, high officials, and politicians.

The rapid adaptation of the social system in the development of new procedures, values, and problems is impossible without a new dynamism pervading the society. This means a new and more open style for all of the public agencies responsible for its management. This also means investment at lower levels of the system, including the fields of job training, employment, and health, as well as regulation of the means of communication, distribution of aid, subsidies and loans to local communities, and the development of education.

A Strategy of Working with Resources and Limitations

I have tried to point out a few concrete aims in order to give an idea of what changes are necessary for bureaucracies to play their part effectively in a society that is in the process of becoming totally different from the one they were designed for. However, it is quite obvious that each of these aims would require large-scale measures to make them work, which cannot be brought to bear. Not that the direct material investment is so costly, but the social, cultural, and intellectual limits are too narrow. To confront the most basic workings of a system as interdependent and solid as our public administration would immediately arouse the opposition of professional, union, and political groups that would be extremely difficult to overcome.

I repeat, the problem of finding a strategy is insoluble if we are only guided by our objectives. We have to take our limitations and resources into account in our thinking. We have to mobilize resources because they are available, make use of a trend or development simply because they are there. This can lead us where we want to go more reliably than can the narrow logic of a priority of objectives. Before I begin with three dimensions of this way of thinking—limits, objectives, and resources—I have to make a few remarks about resources.

In a certain sense, everything about a situation, even a limit can be thought of as a resource. But primarily three things lend themselves in this regard: human potential, the qualities of a system that make it capable of action, and the development or motion of the system. The French administrative system generally has a human potential of very high quality, but it is very poorly used. The key to the success of any reform is to figure out what steps to take to free such potential. Working with human resources is often the best way of fighting against the limits that they represent.

The qualities of an administrative system, which can be relied on to be turned into resources, are the counterparts of weaknesses that were thought to be limitations. It is very important to see how they can be used in a positive fashion. For instance, our deductive and abstract intellectual system keeps us from seeing reality, but it is an extremely useful tool. In a world where the capacity for theorizing plays a very important part, it could become a vital resource. But this offsetting quality is useless as long as it is confined to talk of generalities. It has to be redeemed in concrete actions, in particular areas. The problem of value change can be presented only in terms of concrete cases.

This way of thinking implies that precise, complete, and definitive reforms have to be renounced. Strategy, rather than reform, is most important. The direction in which we want to change cannot be precisely defined in advance, and its form is much less important than is commonly thought. Our choice of reforms to make is going to be based on the strategy we use rather than the other way around. Going straight to the formal elements of reform means starting on the road to technocracy. The really relevant choices will be made visible by first thinking in cost-effective terms and then going on to experimentation and action.

There is a final area of thought for analyzing possible resources. It includes the general development and the more specific and spectacular changes of people and institutions, spontaneous arrangements and ways of doing things. This area is perhaps the most important for working out a strategy. Instead of trying to impose technocratic logic on a system made up of reluctant people, what has to be done is to depend on the independent characteristics of this system. Here again, there is great ambivalence. These very characteristics are at the same time generally the source of expectations that are the most troublesome for the management of the system. Making use of them is the best way of reducing the pressures that make the system helpless. From this point of view, one of the most promising forces seems to me to be the resurgence of the provinces in French society, the change in emotional and moral equilibrium between center and periphery.

From this perspective, three main roads, three main strategies come into relief. The first is to act in the provinces because the provinces are changing, they have resources, and they are where the relations with the surrounding world are in a crisis that could be decisive. The second is to take action to open up the elites. This is the pressure point of the system's operation, and it is possible to mobilize the resources that consist of the young elites. They are sensitive to the deep influence of the outside world. The third is to act on behalf of knowledge. Knowledge has become an essential tool, but French intellectual backwardness is remarkable. In a country like ours, where intellectual values are sacred, it is possible that today's crisis could be a precious opportunity.

These three strategies will be the focus of the three chapters that follow. Then, after a more general consideration of the political dreams and illusions of French society today, I will deal with the last two strategies that seem to me to be required but that the administrative system at present cannot handle: taking action with business and with new services.

5

GAMBLING ON PROVINCIAL REFORM

A Strategy, Not a Reform

Despite its impressive hierarchical resemblance to a well-ordered French garden, the regional administrative apparatus is both confused and compartmentalized. Everyone takes care of everything, but nobody listens to anyone else. The differences of status between levels, between layers in the hierarchy, between official technical specialties are far too strong for people to be able to communicate about their real experiences. The centralization of decision making does not simplify things. On the contrary, every person concerned will be able to exert pressure throughout the countless points of coordination. This leads to confusion that attenuates the compartmentalization a bit but at the same time keeps it going. In spite of an obsession with the interests of society, the functioning of the system resists all attempts at innovation and at its worst rejects everything that is alive. This sort of system is inefficient for the following reasons:

1. Because the difficulty of communication it maintains is a major handicap in a world where qualitative change is going on at an accelerating pace.

2. Because it mobilizes much too small a part of its potential resources but also raises expectations that cannot be satisfied.

3. Because it is incapable of understanding the reality of human relations, and of mobilizing underlying goodwill and thus always catches up too late, at too high a price. It rarely is able to

use the innovations that are worked out in society, even though they have been tried out by its own members.

The leadership has recognized the system's drawbacks for a long time. Even the most diehard defenders of administrative orthodoxy agree that the Parisian bureaucracy has to be untangled, the provinces have to be revitalized, and we have to decentralize. Judging by all the speeches, it would seem that decentralization is the main concern of French politics. Since Liberation or before, antibureaucratic sermons have been legion and attempts at reform countless. Only Voltaire's Hurons or Persians could wonder at this extravagance without being sad. Every politician, Left or Right, even the most strict Jacobin, Gaullist follower of Chirac or Communist, says that he is a "fierce" or at least a "determined" decentralizer.[1] And yet the repeated actions of these same politicians work together to reinforce the restrictions and control of the centralized apparatus. Even their reforms help to stifle the initiatives that come out of the bureaucratic dungeon and the arrangements that practical people have found to cope with it. A politician will reflexively answer "more decentralization" to every question, the way they said "more education" until recently.

I think that the basic mistake is to think in terms of reform first. This means a new distribution of decision-making power, a new arrangement of rights and duties, new ways of doing things, a new formula for distributing resources. We do not need yet another trick reform. The general, definitive, absolute reform that the idealists dream about is impossible. Partial reforms, resulting from compromises between forces at work in the system, however, are likely to make its functioning more burdensome. To have any chance of success, we have to think in terms of strategy, not reform, to give more importance to the development of human relations than to the theory of the state, to have more trust in people than in procedures.

This is not Utopian thinking. Let me remind those who assert that centralization is irreversible that just such a reversal took place in France between 1871 and 1884, at the beginning of the Third Republic. It effectively halted the movement toward centralization begun by the constitution of the Napoleonic state and for fifty years pushed France into a slow but uninterrupted and very efficient movement toward decentralization. The greatest period of local democracy France has ever known was due to this reversal of a trend. Why did it stop? This is one of the critical questions that should concern our historians. The social, political, and even economic development of France during the last fifty years cannot be understood without answering it. The great depression of the 1930s, the ordeal of Vichy and the Occupation, the political conditions of the Liberation and reconstruction, are all factors to be considered but are not enough to provide an answer. Although we do not yet understand the reasons for this regression, we should not give up on doing anything. There is no reason why we should not be capable of going on now to a trend reversal such as the one our great-grandparents accomplished.

What Is Involved

Taking action in the provinces means attacking provincial administration, which includes the services of the prefects and what are called the external services of the state, or the body of officials of the various ministries who are in the field to provide more or less directly to those administered. What is involved is much more important than may appear, less because of the sum total of activities involved than because of their psychological and political impact. Provincial administration is not dramatic and not involved with "big" policies. But the fundamental balance of French society is maintained through it, and French citizens find in it the social support they need for individual activity. The citizen affirms his belonging to and participation in running a community through (and sometimes against) this provincial administration.

What is provincial administration in practice? It does not include all public affairs because many things are not under its control. First among these are defense, foreign affairs, and justice. Then, less clearly perhaps, comes the area of finance, which hardly anyone wants to stop being a responsibility of the nation. Finally come the big public services of an industrial nature—post office, telecommunications, arms procurement, the tobacco monopoly—which serve the whole society and not just territorial units. As big as these exceptions are, particularly in the number of people they employ, they do not include an extraordinary number of rich and diverse activities. To list at random, these include urban renewal and facilities, housing, roads, job training, employment, social welfare, environment, recreation, and culture. One final problem I will not deal with right away, and that is education, which in France has taken on a nationwide character in spite of its local base.

These activities have three things in common. First, they are mainly concerned with expenditures of money. Of course, they do build, operate, and manage things, but from the point of view of the Ministry of Finance, the principal task of the administrations in charge of them is to distribute funds. Second, their functions can be carried out by people of other public offices. That is relatively rare in France, in contrast to England or Germany, but even here towns and departments manage many of the developments built with state money. Agricultural professionals run their own subsidized schools, and in the field of health the cooperation of the state, municipalities, and the medical profession leads to highly unusual personnel management. And finally there are functions that, to succeed, can and should bring nonadministrative activities into play, since they thrive on a network of complex relationships. For the sectors like recreation, culture, sports, and training, it is clear that the official cannot accomplish anything without depending on professionals, to whom he must often defer. But it is the same for agriculture and should be the same for environment and employment.

The factors at play in these activities have been thrown into turmoil by their extremely rapid recent evolution. Over the last twenty years, it is important to point out, provincial administration has been dominated by the problems of investment. To keep pace with urban evolution, the rate of increase in expenses has grown dramatically. In this kind of inflationary climate, officials had much to offer and could influence local leaders by advising them of the policy that was the easiest to subsidize. These years of inflation were also years of centralization. This trend has now reversed. The bulk of investments has been made, the demographic revolution has stopped, and we are feeling the reverberations of the financial crisis. From now on the cost of operations will be the key element. The cost of managing facilities, which was minimized during their construction, now appears much heavier than was foreseen. The white paper, *Les Grandes villes devant leur avenir*, published in 1977 by the Society of Big City Mayors, gives some arresting examples. The consequences of personnel limitations are becoming increasingly visible. Along with the cost of operations, there has appeared a change in the relation between investment and the services actually provided, between services provided and the tangible results. Everything costs far more than had been thought because nothing is suited to the actual situation. To get something done, resources must be mobilized in different programs and services that have different policies, and principles must be made to cooperate.

Hence there is a necessity to decompartmentalize, to deprofessionalize, or at least, to limit the field of administrative professionalism. In this area we need less "gentle growth" than administrative craftsmanship. Administrative coordination is too expensive and is not effective. Multiple skills seem to be the only solution in many cases. The movement against professional bureaucracies started by Ivan Illich has certainly led to some stances that are too radical and that are untenable in the long run. But as a reaction against the cancer-like growth of the official apparatus, it is fundamentally healthy and extremely useful for shaking the smugness of the professionals. If we left them to develop their operations as they see them, they would always demand that the rest of society be organized according to their aims.

The main job that awaits us in administrative development is how to rediscover quality along with true demand on the basis of practice. Nowhere is this task as urgent as in regional administration. This is the priority area for trying new approaches because bureaucratic professionalism, inflation, and waste cannot be fought without some means of synthesis, control, and reflection that are close to actual experience. This includes feedback, communication, and participation by consumers and citizens, all of which relate to local politics. And provincial administration is where a new kind of management can start to develop, with the expertise and organizing functions that are indispensable for this feedback.

Today's system cannot succeed because it does not contain a political force that can demonstrate strongly enough the demand for synthesis, decompartmentalization, and deprofessionalization that citizens feel. But a new deal is all the more to be hoped for because all the elements are there for it to succeed, the objective needs, as well as the human resources and social movement in this direction.

The System of Notables Is the Obstacle

The provincial administrative system is not abstract and inhuman. Contrary to stereotype, it is not based on the exclusion of politicians and on the helpless dependence of those in the provinces. Instead it closely links local elected officials and notables in working out and applying decisions. But it really is a restrictive system in which the relationship with the civil society around it is organized around a limited number of privileged contacts. It is democratic, but in its access rather than in its responsibilities. It is more important for it to guarantee equitable and fair treatment to everyone than to support group initiatives. For the former, it has to set up routes of access on which privileges and restrictions are constantly being imposed. This means the suppression of all attempts at mobilization and social innovation because they go against both its egalitarian principles and elitist practices.

I have already referred to the sociological context and power relations that link up local elected officials (mayor, assemblyman, town councillor, presidents of the chamber of commerce, farmers' council, craftsman's council) with the administrative officials (regional equipment administrator, bureau chief, or departmental director of the prefecture). I think this point has to be underlined because the usual analysis rests on a totally false view of the provincial political and administrative system. Two studies, done six years apart and based on a large sample of notables and officials in very different departments, provide very clear-cut information on this point. Communication is much easier between notables and officials who are partners in their roles than between the main levels of the administrative pyramid. Despite the opposition and complaints he arouses, a local highway administrator communicates better with the local notables than with his superior, the departmental director of equipment.[2]

Elected officials are perfectly willing to accept the requirements of the general interest imposed by administrators, who internalize the electoral concerns of the former. The local notable, as we have said, is often remarkably expert in administrative technique, and the administrator in turn becomes a local notable. Between them develops a complicity based on common experience, complementary interests, and identical requirements. This complicity, which does not entirely rule out conflicts, can be found at various levels, depending on the characteristics of the administrative pyramid involved. But it is particularly crucial at the department level, which is the essential level for this integration.

This paradoxical relationship shows up clearly upon analysis of the way in which decisions are made. No one who is responsible can make a decision by himself. He first has to arrive at a compromise with those counterparts that may be affected by his decision. Up to that point, there is nothing unexpected. But the characteristic rule of this administrative world is the tacit or informal rule that a compromise is never directly negotiated between the parties involved. Instead it takes place through the intervention of a pressure group or a person who does not belong to the group or the office of the parties concerned. The functions of integration and coordination are always carried out by someone whose activity or source of authority is different from those of the groups, offices, or interests that he integrates. The coordinator often tends to impose a preconceived solution that takes the interests concerned into account but that was worked out without any real negotiation, under the guise of another rationale—technical specifications, local traditions, and the interests of society at large. Here, contrary to common belief, the coordinator is not necessarily a nonspecialized official, nor is he necessarily an official at all. A well-established notable can often impose a compromise needed by bureaucracies that cannot see eye to eye.

Although these general chracteristics of the system are very important, two completely different models, the rural model and that of big cities, must be distinguished.

The Rural Model
The most traditional pattern has two levels, that of village mayors and departmental "notables". The notables are those who "accumulate" power by holding several different public offices at the same time, mayors of chief towns, or departmental representatives. The officials who matter are those who work in the field (tax collectors, local highway administrators) and departmental directors of external services.

The mayor is all powerful when it comes to integrating the interests of everyone in his commune. The people have faith in him because the only way for a commune to fend for itself in a democracy based on contacts is to have a stable mayor. But he is largely powerless to undertake positive action because he has no financial resources of his own and no independent technical experts at his disposal. This means that he has to get technical support, subsidies, and loan authorizations that only officials can provide. This puts him in a subordinate position in relation to them, which is reinforced by the fact that the official is always confronting several mayors who are competing with one another.[3] The official can use this competition to keep them all dependent on him.

But if the official has power over the mayors, he does not impose power arbitrarily on them. He knows that he will be judged by his capacity to settle disagreements without conflict and takes into account the possible reactions of local politics. The most important notables are those who have their contacts in the prefecture and in Paris and who can give him their necessary support in this manner. Thus the mayor depends on the official, and the official on the prominent notable. The notable is the product of an essential characteristic of the political system, the possibility of holding a plurality of elective offices that has in fact become the norm. To have a political career, a person must hold several offices; it is this accumulation that makes a person a notable.

This is part and parcel of the system. In an organization where communication is difficult, those who are at the focal point of communication become key people. This is clearly the case of the politician who holds a plurality of elective offices at various levels of the hierarchy. The different interactions in which he can intervene are independent, and he can use his influence in one to bring pressure to bear on his contacts in another. An elected official who has this superior power can use his influence in a much pleasanter and more sympathetic way than a traditional potentate. He can repay his friends without punishing his enemies too harshly and without arousing public displeasure. The bureaucracy, which needs him, bestows many favors on him. If he is skillful, he can take advantage of this and play the role of the conciliator, the coordinator, the prominent notable whom everyone needs. In return, an overwhelming majority of the mayors who hold several elected offices espouse the views of officialdom and are totally identified with the system. Ninety-one percent of this type of mayor assert that officials do not hesitate to defend local interests against Paris. This is in contrast to only 60 percent of the mayors who do not hold a plurality of elective offices. Seventy-five percent of the first type of mayor add that there are too many people who interfere, and 70 percent of officials say the same thing.[4]

The Urban Model

In the big cities, the same formal and informal rules produce entirely different results, for a very simple reason. In the urban system there are no more small-town mayors, and there is only one level in the political system. Consequently the field official does not have to face minor elected officials, who represent the population very well but can be manipulated easily simply by playing them off against each other. With elected officials, the situation is reversed. Instead of manipulating the small-town mayors by dealing with the influence of the notables, he is more or less dependent on the big city mayor, against whom his only protection is the bureaucratic rule of law. The big city mayor, who is in a position to integrate local interests as well as resolve differences among bureaucrats, becomes a boss, much more than any other person in French political life. His power is the result of his being an intermediary between the local grass roots and the Paris-centered administrative system. His position is a favorable one in a democracy of contacts, but he is dependent on it. He has the power of the lone man who can negotiate more freely, but he also has his weakness. He has more difficulty because it is harder for him to mobilize human resources that could pose a threat to him.

In any case, the power of the mayor brings at best only indirect benefits for the citizens. The citizen has no understanding of the interaction among insiders. The presence of other prominent notables, whether colleagues, allies, or adversaries, who counterbalance the power of the mayor serve only to complicate the decision-making mechanism without any benefit for him. Although he is far superior to the rural citizen as far as culture and information are concerned, the urban citizen is in fact much less aware of what is going on than is his compatriot in the countryside. Surveys show that he is much more bitter and alienated. Today's municipal reforms will not be able to change much in the workings of these basic mechanisms.

It is thus the system that is problematic rather than each of its individual mechanisms. And it would certainly be a mistake to think that its drawbacks can be eliminated without affecting its good points. It cannot be transformed without calling into question the advantages that make it strong. If it has to be changed, though, this is because the balance between advantages and disadvantages is not favorable, and today's trend is leading to an increasing deterioration.

Gambling on the provinces does not mean pitting the provinces against Paris but rather relying on grass roots forces that can transform the provincial system. What is the obstacle to this happening? Essentially it is this honeycomb-like decision-making and power system, which involves officials and notables in an exclusive relationship. It protects public affairs from intrusion by citizens and creates and maintains the interaction of favors and privileges, the stability and conservatism of the elites, and the compartmentalization of competing units.

In a system based on equality of distribution, participants can gain only at somebody else's expense. It is in their interests, therefore, to isolate themselves, to adopt a defensive attitude, and to communicate as little as possible. Their problems can be solved by cross-control mechanisms, but this only makes competition and noncommunication more tolerable and does not eliminate its disadvantages. In any case, the positions allowing these conciliatory compromises have to be few and stable, and this leads to elitism. Democracy by contacts, no matter what is done, cannot bring about communication, the exchange of experiences, active partnerships, positive initiatives, and innovation.

But it is still very strong because until now it maintained the equality of participants with evenhandedness, tolerance, and honesty, because it was still human and understanding. Sadly, this is less and less true, except in rural areas, and this is what makes it more and more vulnerable. Democracy by contacts has withstood rapid urban development and the accompanying inflation of expenses fairly well. Of course, the system was late in getting started, proved to be costly, and led to many technocratic mistakes. But it more or less accomplished its task without too much protest from the people involved. It is adapting much less well now to the very growth that it helped to steer in a technocratic direction. The imbalance between city and country, between the urban and rural patterns, is difficult to put up with. It is the cause of the civic alienation of much of our population. It evokes their hostility not only against the administrative system but against all social control. In the end it becomes only an irritant, and more and more problems escape its control. It is incapable of putting forth new resources, initiatives, and understanding. Technocratic mechanisms take up the slack in planning, industrial development, and employment, not to mention professional management. Agriculture is the only successful example of this, but it encourages imitations.

The last and perhaps the most important problem is that the inescapable demand for quality that naturally follows from the quantitative inflation of the last twenty years will pose more and more insoluble problems. This leads both to the dangers of deterioration and the opportunities for change that are discernible in the contemporary unrest.

The Region Is the Best Choice

How is it possible to budge a system that is so stubborn but so deeply rooted in the fabric of society? Even if our seemingly modest aim is only to reverse the trend, the job seems impossible at first. The forces and resources exist, but they are engaged in different ways. And besides there is no way to get a grip on the system. The whole problem of a strategy for change is how to find this hand hold. Among the sensitive points of the system, one must be chosen upon which the mobilization of resources can most easily be brought about.

Let us try to work out the minimum goals we want to attain. What is necessary to reverse the trend? I think that to do the job three points must be unblocked. First, democratic deliberative institutions enjoying strong legitimacy have to be set up around several responsibilities that are clearly perceived by the public. A new system can develop around such institutions in order to counterbalance and correct the system of democracy by contacts. Second, the system of notables has to be substantially opened up, in such a way that a stronger competition among people for a larger number of positions will ensure sufficient turnover and a public debate over real choices. Power can be fought only with power, and the only way to overthrow exclusiveness, hierarchy, and secrecy is by increasing the number of notables. Finally, positive partnerships have to develop, which will enable common undertakings to break up the compartmentalization of provincial units and areas of action.

We have to find out what measure or reform will allow us to carry out these unblocking actions with enough support from the available forces and resources. The first suggestion that arises is that this reform has to be a political one, creating a new legitimacy. No reform that is purely administrative, no rearrangement of the powers in existence now can do this. In the present framework of legitimacy, it is impossible to escape the pressure of the flawless chain of command that links the bottom and the top of the civil service in an endless pyramid. It might be objected that notables do manage to penetrate this chain. It is true that they have access to it, but only if they can find such a secure niche for themselves that they become part of it. They give it a local legitimacy, and in return it gives them a recognition that amounts to a sort of nationwide legitimacy.

It might be said that the creation of autonomous local political forces would be a veritable revolution against the central government. Not at all. Many developed countries have institutions that confine competing authorities, and they manage very well. The United States, Germany, and Japan have regularly elected regional institutions. Even in France, the situation that has existed since the Third Republic, with its departmental councils, has carried the embryo of competing autonomous authority. In the final analysis, it is not such a tremendous upheaval to go from local administration to local government. The French are perfectly capable of this, and in many respects they show a great feeling for local government. There remains the decisive problem of where to locate this political entity. The reform to be carried out should cause as little trauma as possible but should create a power with sufficient weight, located at a point in the administrative chain of command, that will let it lead to a real break with the past.

In the present state of French society, only the region meets these criteria. The region's long administrative gestation period has prepared the ground well enough for its political legitimacy to be recognized without overthrowing the Republic. A regional deliberative body would have enough weight to break up the exclusive control over networks of contacts with Paris, at least those in several important areas of continuity. The region today seems to be the prime administrative unit capable of developing the sort of group solidarity appropriate for a highly developed society, mainly because only at this level will a real cohesion between town and country be able to take place.

How is it possible to establish such an autonomous political body? I would make a proposal in terms that, curiously enough, are disturbing to French political tradition, but whose meaning would seem unremarkable anywhere else: an assembly elected by direct, universal suffrage. From the very beginning, this was the logical consequence of regional development. But up to now our political leaders have moved backward just when they were about to take this decisive step. This deep reluctance deserves attention. On the one hand, it is said that the election of a regional assembly would not solve anything, that it would mean adding yet another factor to the already immense administrative confusion, and that the region is too remote to deal with practical human problems but too small to have a role in economic matters. In short, it is said that this reform would lack real impact and is not worth carrying out. On the other hand, the spector of the dismantling of the state and the nation is raised, and France is supposedly not strong enough to let the provinces come to life again. French unity, which was so painstakingly created in the course of a thousand years of history, should not be called into question by such regionalist fantasies. Many politicians use these two contradictory lines of argument at the same time.

As for the second argument, it is absurd to think that a regional election could threaten as ancient and cohesive a nation as France; Germany, for example, a much more recently created nation, does not suffer the slightest harm from its federal structure. And as for the first argument, a regional assembly must not be thought of as a technocratic instrument for resolving low-level problems or problems of economic policy. Its real relevance is strategic, since it aims to create deliberative bodies and relations of interdependence that are free of administrative control.

What other possibilities are there? The first is obvious: the department. At first glance it could be revived without having to create a new institution. This was the choice of President Pompidou and Alain Peyrefitte. But it does not appear that much progress has been made beyond very sincere assertions of principle because the choice of the department presents insuperable difficulties. For a long time, the department has been the mainstay of democracy by contacts. It constitutes a cumbersome administrative structure that is deeply rooted in a long history. It is overlaid by a network of notables who are not strong but whose honeycomb-like compartmentalization makes them very resistant to change. The departmental council is a deliberative body made up of the foremost notables. In addition, it suffers from being elected in a deplorable way. Rural cantons usually have a majority of its seats, even though they include what is often a minority of the population. Regarding cities, negotiations take place outside the departmental system anyway, and big city mayors live effortlessly side by side with a departmental council that does not concern them in the slightest.

For the department to have a real deliberative body, a drastic reform of the system of representation would be necessary, which would run afoul of the notables and the officials of the prefecture. It would also be necessary to reintegrate the cities into the departments, which is not as simple as it seems. If they were represented equitably in the departmental councils, the countryside and small towns would be overwhelmed by the big cities. Finally, it is much easier to set up a regional assembly in which town and country could build up a new and fruitful solidarity than to try to square the circle in a framework that has become totally inappropriate for responsible democracy. Moreover, from a sociological point of view it is always preferable to build a movement on an institution created from scratch rather than transform an old institution upon which old ways of doing things weigh heavily.

Another possibility might be the cities and municipalities, which are more human and which also enjoy the general support of public opinion. This was essentially the choice made by President Giscard d'Estaing, after some hesitation, at the beginning of his term. In my opinion, this is the choice of a planner and not a strategic choice. The commune is certainly closer to the citizen than the department or the region is. It is also true that as many decisions as possible should be made at this grass-roots level, which is most suitable for democratic participation. But the problem is not how to make decisions local; it lies in the system that produces the decisions. In the present system, municipal decisions are not the concern of the people; it is not good policy for a well-informed mayor to have the people participate. The mayor has power because he is the only viable contact with the administrative system. To keep it, he has to remain the indispensable intermediary, and this requires social distance, secrecy, and no participation by citizens. The present-day system is actually one of government at two levels. Universal suffrage chooses a small number of leaders, who then organize a decision-making system among themselves that is more or less closed. Far from being a holdover from the past, this separation is growing larger. The spread of confederations of communes, the recent start of a council of urban areas, and regional councils are examples of this, not to mention plans for making municipalities out of cantons.[5]

Thus, opting for the commune means going against the present decision-making system. Contrary to popular belief, this would be extremely difficult, since the mayors do not have the slightest interest in changing a system that protects them so well. The administrative and decision-making systems, being what they are, there is hardly any likelihood that the mayors would accept this poisoned apple without a murmur. They are being given a phony decentralization in today's reform of local communities. Of course, they will not oppose it openly and will seek to take advantage of it. But it will not help them to develop local democracy, nor will it help to free them from external control. The town council would have to become a real deliberative body, capable of working out policy. The mayors of today are too weak to put up with such an encroachment on their power. In any case, nobody is thinking of doing this.

From this point of view, the election of a regional assembly by universal suffrage would be a much more powerful stimulus than the elimination of formal controls. Such a reform goes to the very heart of the system of notables. But one indispensable condition is that holding a plurality of elective offices must be prohibited.[6] Only such a prohibition can lead to the accomplishment of the second of the objectives, the enlargement of the circle of notables and the introduction of competition into this closed circle. This prohibition makes no sense unless it is based on a new source of authority, and in the present system, such a measure would not enlarge the circle but would only complicate the existing machinery. If it were associated with the creation of a new assembly that had great authority, the same measure would bring about a substantial renewal of the existing elites. It would be a new test for political responsibilities and would lead the present notables to play a very different game. Faced with a system that was more alive from the point of view of democratic legitimacy, the mayors of small and medium towns would very quickly feel the need to rely on a less passive electorate. Big city mayors would become more vulnerable to a reform that the growth of their responsibilities has required for a long time but that has been stymied by the confusion of the system.

What will become of financial problems? I would like to give General de Gaulle's answer: those responsible will have to follow. To me, it seems almost impossible for the Ministry of Finance to accept giving up very little in the present system, just as it is hard to imagine their refusing to accept the necessary amount of financial autonomy for regions that are based on strong assemblies. Of course, we must begin at some point, with the right to levy a minimum of taxes. But once this right is recognized, the natural growth of activity should lead to a gradual change in the balance of resources.

Aside from setting up agendas and regulating the length of meetings, I think there is one last essential condition for a new system to be able to develop around an assembly elected by universal suffrage. It must be allowed to hire a minimum staff of qualified personnel. At the same time that they take over administrative activities that are now centralized, the regions should take over the personnel who carry them out. From the beginning, it is essential that regions have at their disposal high-quality consultants under contract: experts, organizers, and politicians who can try new ideas with their new regulative functions.

I have intentionally left aside two questions that have been the focus of attention for too long: the nature of the regional executive and the status of the department in a regional framework. Neither seems to me to be at a point where it can be dealt with. I think that if the strategy of decentralization is seriously undertaken, the withering away of the department has to be accepted as inevitable. The department has meaning only as an organ of the central government, and because of the town-country opposition it cannot be democratically reformed. This gradual eclipse will take time because right now the department fulfills an irreplaceable function in its responsibility for rural administration. Why not let it retain this responsibility? At the same time, a start can be made at trying new arrangements for the canton, the neighborhood, or the old boroughs.

I think that the problem of the executive could also be resolved through experience. The law of 1871 on the departmental councils facilitated real decentralization for at least fifty years, despite the retention of the prefects. Therefore it is not absolutely necessary for a regional assembly that is stronger than the departmental councils of the Third Republic to be able to create its own executive. I do not think that French society is ready for such a step, which is psychologically difficult. This is unfortunate, but for the moment a compromise that would maintain the function of the prefect in relation to an assembly that would be master of its own agenda should be enough to reverse the direction in which things are going.

The Significance of This Approach

Readers might be disappointed with this outline of strategy. It is only a partial sketch that does not allow a precise definition of the rights and duties of each partner, and it leaves the most basic distribution of power in limbo. It does not seem to be strong enough for its ambitions, and yet it is too strong to fail to arouse hostility.

I am well aware of all that. However, I have presented this sketch only as an essay on strategy rather than as a program for the reform and planning of the political and administrative apparatus. A strategy for change both allows for flexibility and contradictions and must also be based on a small measure of imbalance. In this case disequilibrium is a creative force. On occasion, only ambiguity can unite partners who have different points of view; only flexibility can lead them along a common path. Experience will settle things, and through experience resources will have been mobilized. In this way it is to be hoped that in the end the array of forces will have been changed enough for progress to be made.

Rather than be criticized as an incomplete reform, the strategy I have presented should be considered in terms of the approach it uses. What is this approach? It is a "new deal." If the cards are shuffled well enough, the game will change, it is to be hoped, and a new cycle of change can begin. Is this realistic? I think that the possibilities for success are at hand because the human resources are there. Of course, provincial leaders are not as loud in their demands for the creation of regions as they were fifteen years ago. This is because these leaders, who have no political and few civic opportunities, partially mobilized in favor of creating regions, which was the first experiment, and were disappointed. Some of them then transferred their hopes to socialism and were disappointed again. Their communities give them only a narrow area of activity, and I think it is clear that they would make full use of a real opportunity on a regional level if it were offered to them. As soon as a strict enough law prohibiting the holding of a plurality of elected offices forces the notables to make a choice, a profound renewal of the political milieu will take place. The rise of new notables, new strata, to use the nineteenth-century term, would be both the condition for the success of the strategy of decentralization and its first result.

Opponents of change greatly fear that local leadership will be of poor quality. They can cite endless examples to emphasize the irresponsibility, the shortsightedness, and tastelessness of the notables. For them it would be a tremendous risk to allow the notables a free hand. What is forgotten is that the Parisian administrative elite, not the notables, sets the pattern of high-rise apartments and reinforced concrete. What is forgotten in particular is that if the personnel at the departmental level are often of poor quality (which is an argument in favor of developing the regions), the system itself is responsible for the decline. The decline, measured by comparing the Parisian city council at the turn of the century with that of today, cannot be attributed to the backwardness of life in Paris. The "new deal" will make new elites arise and will revive the ones who are already there. The latter are as timid and stingy as they are only because right now it is the best game for them to play. Let me make another reference to the reversal of centralization a century ago. The Third Republic had no trouble finding responsible elites. Traditional notables and new social strata provided high-quality leadership to a society that was bourgeois but active and proud of its local accomplishments. I cannot believe that we could not do as well with the far superior potential in human resources and knowledge available today.

Furthermore, some very dramatic changes have taken place in the last twenty years. Let us take two typical examples, those of Brittany and Champagne. In Champagne, the department of the Marne, which had been fairly poor in agriculture, managed to capture first place in per-capita agricultural income. At the same time, industrial production grew substantially, and the general growth of its population and employment were among the highest in all of France. What was the cause of this? It was due to the dogged persistence of local elites, who had taken on the responsibility for an immense effort involving technical and job training and investments at the local level. True, they could count on the help of dedicated officials, but the officials followed rather than led the movement. The same change took place, even more dramatically, in Nord-Finistère, which was totally transformed from top to bottom by the effect of what in this case was personal rather than collective leadership. In the light of such striking successes, how can we fail to have confidence in the provinces?

At this point, government leaders might raise the objection that there is a danger of disorder and inflation. If all of these programs were allowed to go on at the same time, the system would be overloaded immediately. The same objection was made several years ago when the Germans discovered the dangers of inflation inherent in spending by the provincial *länder* and other decentralized authorities that were very numerous in comparison with the *länder*. I think that this example is conclusive evidence. The Germans were able to ascertain the regulating procedures that were necessary to respond to this change without reducing local autonomy. Can we not do likewise? There is no cultural characteristic that stands in our way other than the intellectual laziness of our administrative elite, which is incapable of imagining ways of acting that are different from the controls and restrictions it is used to. In this regard, it might even be arguable that the danger of local bungling would be the best stimulus for developing new and more sophisticated modes of government. From this point of view, decentralization is an opportunity that should not be passed up.

Whenever the desire for decentralization begins to be translated into concrete steps, another objection is often raised concerning the quality of life. Local elites, it is feared, will be shortsighted in matters of health, culture, and development, as if only Paris had the ideas, in opposition to the conservative provinces. If local leaders take conservative positions, it is because they have no other immediate choice. Rather, they can accept the long term only with great reservations. Bureaucracies that fiercely protect their principles against poorly educated notables make them insecure and alienated. What the bureaucracies need is to give up their managerial habits and let in the breath of fresh air that only concrete experience can bring. In this way, too, true decentralization would be an opportunity to catch.

Finally, it may be objected that this will lead to the political involvement of the provinces. True, this strategy would lead to the reinvolvement in politics of a hinterland made apathetic by bureaucrats. Would this be bad? Is this not the only way of rebalancing and modifying a nationwide political system that cannot be eliminated in any case? Is this not the only way to change politics itself a little, to unblock a central power that today is mired in impotence and is ideologically alienated? Is this not the only way to diversify a played-out political game, to give to less bureaucratic elites the real means to prove themselves?

6
OPENING UP THE ELITES

Why the Elites?

"Making our elite more democratic" is one of the pious promises that our politicians think that they must ritually utter when they are looking for votes. It would be fruitless to add my voice to this useless chorus. The strategy I am suggesting does not consist of dealing with the social background of the elite, but another one that seems much more critical, in spite of appearances. This is the very notion of the elite itself: the number of its members, the walls that protect them, how they compete with one another, and the exclusive power that they exercise together.

First, what characterizes an elite is its numerical size. Is it broad and composed of a large number of people, or is it small and narrow? Next is its degree of openness. Is it closed off and very difficult to get into, or is it an open elite to which all forms of talent and abilities are allowed access? Finally, there is its competitive nature. Is it a monopolistic caste whose members support one another mutually to safeguard their privileges, or a changing cluster of people, with unclear boundaries in which anyone with ability can compete equally?

My strategy rests on the following simple argument. To a great extent, the difficulty of governing French society, and its inability to adapt and innovate, is due to the closed and exclusive nature of its elite. Changing the elite's class composition would do nothing to make society more efficient and more democratic. Rather the governmental apparatus can be made more efficient and society freer and more equal by opening up the elite and changing its relation to the rest of society.

Is such a turnaround possible? I think that two sets of reasons can be cited to prove that it is. First, today's elite has more and more trouble carrying out its job in a society that is too complicated for the style of action and a mode of government that its social organization imposes on it. The elite are aware of the need for renewal, and the rest of the society vaguely agrees. Moreover the respect attached to the values of intellectual awareness and efficiency by French society, and by the civil service in particular, is a real asset in this regard. Therefore it is possible to open up the elite, and to my way of thinking, this can be crucial for the renewal of French society. This strategy will allow us to undertake a real reform of the state and bureaucracy, as well as the educational system. It can open up the way to the service-oriented and knowledge-oriented society of the future.

This unusual strategy will seem simplistic to some people and surprising or silly to others. How can I seriously believe, they might ask, that we can reform society simply by increasing the number of students at the elite training schools, because this is where the elites are recruited? My answer would be that what is needed is something broader than the reorganization of the elite training schools. These include the elimination of the top civil service caste, the transformation of entry requirements for high public officials, competition among schools, and the change from today's didactic teaching to new forms of learning by fieldwork and independent study. An increase in the number of competitors in the struggle for admissions would be an important step. It would help to smash an outdated monopoly whose consequences are formidable. Today's system makes no use of available human resources, prevents new resources from being sought out, and makes it impossible to alter our hierarchical style of government.

As regards curriculum, my proposals would meet with strong objections. It is generally believed that reform has to be begun at the grade school level, if not in kindergarten, and then be moved up from level to level. As I have shown, I am opposed to this way of thinking, this planning approach to change. It seems logical to start at the bottom, of course, but it is both impossible and poor strategy. It means forgetting that people themselves, with their ability and enthusiasm, are the essential resources for change. A good strategy must first seek to develop these resources and put them in a position where they can take action. It therefore has to start at the top.

Other criticisms will be raised against dealing with civil service through the elite. Why reform what works relatively well—top public offices, the top civil service corps—while there are so many more urgent everyday problems? But my choice is logical and may even be the only possible one in the light of a serious examination of the system that the French civil service represents. True, the competence and devotion of high officials, particularly in the Ministry of Finance, are what makes the system work in spite of the enormous difficulties encountered. Nonetheless the elitist system itself, which assigns exclusive responsibility for resolution of complex societal problems to top officials, is responsible in large part for creating these very problems. For the system to make progress, it seems to me that there is no other choice but to change gradually the terms of a problem that will remain unsolved in its present state.

It might be said that there are many other basic problems, even aside from inflation and unemployment: the distribution of power in society, the role of money, and the quality of life. Notwithstanding these priorities, the foremost concrete problem is action, and for action tools are needed, most important of which is a system of government.

The Present System

Every society produces elites or groups of leaders linked by a network of relations of cooperation and rivalry and capable of eliminating or at least limiting competition through a system of protection and collusion. Liberals can dream of a free market of talent and partisans of self-management may dream of eliminating all inequality, but no society has ever managed to function without an elite. As in so many other areas of social organization, there is no ideal solution. No complex human system can do without the specialized roles of experts and authorities. Some of those who occupy these roles occasionally find it in their individual interest to keep competition open. But if a sufficiently unified group is established, the temptation to take over and impose limitations on entry becomes irresistible. In modern society, the walls around social castes have largely fallen, but control over entry into the elite by diplomas and examinations has taken their place. This is the way elite groups protect themselves against competition, and for society it is an obstacle to change. Even though an elite exists in every social system, there is still a great difference between a society based on the existence of a very narrow elite, even one chosen in an egalitarian fashion, and a society in which the elite has more people in it, is more open, and can recruit new talent more widely.

In France today, in spite of what meets the eye, there is a very restrictive situation in the administrative world and in large areas of activity that are directly linked to it. In a sense, all positions are equally open to people with talent; the honesty of the qualifying examinations is very widely known. But there is a monopoly, which one might think was eliminated by this, that reappears at least as strongly in another form. Very small social groups are established that have a near monopoly on a certain number of positions because they organize the selection process. True, this is no longer a question of social castes, but these artificial groups established by the selection process itself—such as the Elite Corps of Finance Inspectors and the Mining Engineers—behave in the same restrictive fashion. A hallmark of the French public administrative system is that most of its executive positions are, to all intents and purposes, restricted to graduates of two elite training schools: the Polytechnic School and the National School of Administration. But the selection process does not stop there. The only graduates of these schools with a good chance of success are those whose official standing in the class has won them access to a prestigious administrative or technical corps. There is an almost formal hierarchy that distinguishes the members of the top administrative corps from those who have less prestige. The specialized abilities of each corps, as well as their history and organization, make for a distribution of positions that further restricts competition.

This system extends to various nationalized sectors of industry, whose top positions as a rule are permanently reserved for members of the top administrative and technical corps. It may not influence all private business, but it does have a large effect on certain big businesses in sectors traditionally tied to the state, of which the steel industry may be the best example. Similar systems govern other areas of activity that are subject to the market, such as health, education, and architecture. Finally, although the center of the problem is at the top, this system has also worked its way downward. The successive layers of upper- and middle-level enclosures exert a pressure that brings about conditions of competition and status that replicate the pattern at the top.

How has this situation been allowed to develop and persist? Because of the fact that, aside from its drawbacks, it has some substantial advantages, particularly these three. (1) This type of selection procedure allows for the rapid promotion of young, dynamic, brilliant people to important positions. Without it, promotion by seniority would likely prevail. The top administrative corps are a reservoir and a garden for talent. (2) Small elite groups, scattered throughout various offices of regulation and responsibility, are networks of mutual acquaintances and communication that are very dense and powerful, through which many problems of coordination are worked out and essential arrangements are set up. (3) Finally, the qualifying examinations are a very important source of legitimacy, which is the basis for the right to command and guarantee the security and freedom needed to take risks to those in power. Because of its elite, the French civil service can take initiatives.

But these advantages have a very high price, and lead to disastrous side effects. First, although the system does permit young people to rise rapidly to positions of great responsibility, these brilliant people are not necessarily dynamic. In fact, the system fosters conformity because the narrower and more restrictive the group, the greater the group pressure. Elites that are too closed off tend to be arrogant and conformist. In France this tendency is reinforced by the fact that one of the basic assets of many of these groups consists of the mastery of a formal and codified specialty. Finally, although this rapid rise to positions of responsibility provides good experience in business, it tends to protect those whom it benefits from experience that is deeper than what is acquired on the job.

There is another serious drawback: the overly homogeneous nature of these groups and the lack of intellectual cross-fertilization that only diverse origins and upbringing bring about. The system for recruiting the corps prohibits cross-breeding, which seems to be increasingly necessary for developing new ways of doing things. And elite communication networks are not the best solution for the problem of communication among bureaucracies. They tend to deteriorate into rival clans that ruthlessly tear one another down in the struggle for positions and responsibilities. The Byzantine war between the alumni of the Polytechnic School and the National School of Administration is only the most visible example of this.

And finally the solidity of the small elite at the top has a harmful effect on the lower levels, both because they imitate the elite, even in its bad habits, and because they try instinctively to immobilize it. Homogeneity engenders mutual confidence and the establishment of a common language, but it reinforces a deep distrust of outsiders. Communication becomes difficult between the elite and the subordinate groups it needs to enact its decisions. The isolation that protects the elite also maintains an atmosphere of frustration. Contacts between the people who have the ideas and those who carry them out are rare and full of conflict.

More fundamentally, the most serious effect of the system lies in the role that the existence of these elites plays in the maintenance and development of the bureaucratic pattern of government. The two basic characteristics of the pattern, stratification and centralization, are directly tied to the elite's mode of organization. This is clear in the case of stratification. The whole system is structured by the influence of the values that prevail at the top. In the last thirty years, the movement toward more stratification has grown in all parts of the administrative system. Lower-level offices, one after another, have succeeded in adapting the model prevailing at the top for their own use and have imposed it on others. Centralization is associated with the elite system in a much more functional way. In effect, it means hierarchy and command and therefore places greater value on a national elite and devalues local leaders, organizers, and entrepreneurs. Elites themselves are justified only by the enormous weight that centralization exerts at the top. Their whole way of thinking and acting, their very relation to reality, are shaped around this basic responsibility, which in fact is totally artificial. Their philosophy says that no decision may be made unless it is protected by distance and by virtue of an outside and supposedly superior position. This justifies both the elite's existence and centralization at the same time. One cannot be changed without changing the other.

There is a final element linked to the organization of the elite. The French civil service's way of thinking impersonally, abstractly, and deductively, which it has in common with lawmakers, engineers, and economists, exerts a restrictive control over its performance and potential. The training for the top qualifying examinations, and then the elite training schools themselves, perpetuate this pattern of thought. They can do this only because there is a very close correspondence between centralized administrative organization and the way the elite is organized. A way of thinking and a type of rationality do not develop simply as products of an education. They maintain their strength only if they work well in the activities of those who have learned them. They work well, only if they match styles of organization and relations between people.

Such a system restricts innovation to elites that are out of touch with experience and whose overly close interaction with power makes them tend to be conformists. It is no longer defensible in a world in which innovation has become decisive in all areas of human activity, especially in managing and governing the social fabric.

The Two Most Sensitive Points of the System

As I have said, in any strategy of change, the decision regarding where to intervene is critical. It must be an important focal point for regulating the system, and it must at the same time offer opportunities for breaking with the past and initiating development. These vulnerable points have the apparently contradictory characteristics of also being the best protected. But this seems to me to be true of the elite system. It dominates the crucial focal points of control of the political, economic, and certainly the administrative system. It is the key component of the educational system. It functions in the social system the way regulation or programming mechanisms operate in biological systems. Or to use another analogy, it functions in the same way as the mechanisms used by financiers who control an immense empire with only 1 percent of the real capital. If these mechanisms are changed, the whole financial empire or biological system is affected. And it is much easier to do this than to rebuild this empire or system directly, which would be a totally utopian undertaking. The transformation of the elite system, therefore, can have tremendous consequences. At the same time, even though it appears invulnerable, it has two very sensitive points on which pressure can be exerted: the elite training schools and the top administrative corps. These two systems are actually relatively simple and are entirely in the hands of public authorities. To affect them, it is necessary to change neither the law nor the economic system.

The system of the training schools controls access to the world of the elite in a very simple but delicate fashion. It is simple because it imposes an impersonal, seemingly natural limitation on the number of people admitted, which determines the nature of the elite and certain types of competition that take place within it. It is delicate because it goes beyond this crude method for artificially refining the elite. Because of a subtle mixture of hierarchy and compartmentalization of the schools, thanks to an extremely well-protected market of talent and ability and ensure both the high quality of its products—young graduates—and a striking match between supply and demand. It is also delicate from a cultural point of view. The intellectual mold to which the young elite has been subjected is all the more powerful because it is perfectly adjusted both to the characteristics of the administrative functions and to basic cultural tendencies of the bureaucracy.

The system of the top administrative corps dominates everything that has to do with politics, business, power, or money. In this club, or rather these clubs, all of the options and deals are discussed. Not that there is a secret government behind the official one. But whatever parties are in power, whatever their problems, the small circle of people who can be called on to carry out decisions plays a more basic role than current theories about what policy should be followed. The elite corps system maintains and develops the habits of compartmentalization and hierarchy begun by the schools. The corps, of course, are better protected than the schools, and it would be difficult to attack them alone, but it is possible to get at them through a more wide-ranging reform. First, let us examine what it is about the elite training schools that makes them the first thing to change in order to open up, renew, and revitalize the French elite.

The Reform of the Elite Training Schools

The problem is more difficult than may appear, for one simple reason. These schools are a series of legally independent institutions, each with its own charter, its own resources, and a support network that gets its strength from former students and certain exclusive preserves. But at the same time they make up a cohesive system. The same clientele is available to them in undifferentiated fashion, and together they produce a social elite group that is hierarchical but compact, even in their competitive relations. It would be fruitless to want to reform them one by one; obstacles would pile up, and the cohesiveness of the system would always threaten to compromise the results. Conversely an attempt at total overhaul would lead reformers in the direction of abstract and inefficient planning. As in the case of the regional strategy, it seems to me that the solution should be sought in the creation of new institutions. Only through them is it possible for a new dynamic to appear. Therefore the aim should not be the modernization or democratization of the schools, their teaching, or their laws and status, but the transformation of the system that they comprise.

The system of elite training schools is monopolistic. Their diversity and autonomy does not lead to real competition between them because the agencies they supply require specialization and because of the hierarchy in recruiting their students. There are certainly cases of strict monopoly, such as that of the National School of Administration, which recuits only from a population of students who are already specialized. Most of the time, though, they attract the same population, which is distributed hierarchically according to the results of the entrance examinations, and each school thereafter channels its students toward specific careers. This elegant system reduces the tensions that competition would evince from its institutions and spares students the inconvenience of having to choose. But its drawbacks are immense. Not only does it not teach students to make personal decisions, which implies freedom and taking chances, but it obliges them to abide by the most conformist choices. Moreover it brings in an outdated hierarchy of professions and specialties. This makes cooperation much more difficult and freezes the elite into a hierarchical intellectual model that largely sterilizes all capacity for research and experimentation.

The basic problem of the schools is that of selection. What is important for each is not the content of the instruction given to the student, still less is it the experience it permits him to acquire. It is to keep its rank, which means to continue to attract the best students. This rank is assigned by a tradition whose aura has remained strong enough for it to be maintained without too much use of the imagination. It can even be seen that the pressure of the old boys, which in practice is an essential element of governance, is most often exercised in a conservative way. Hence the weakness of the elite training schools in research and development, their intellectual dullness, and their conformity. Even the research laboratories of the Polytechnic School are so cut off from teaching activity that the usefulness of their association with the school is in question. Of course, there are notable exceptions, such as the School of Mines in Paris.[1] But it is remarkable that none of our schools has succeeded in being, or even sought to be, an intellectual center comparable to those which for many years the best Western universities have been. It is sad to see how poorly these institutions make use of their extraordinary resources: the intellectual capital of a long and glorious tradition, a student body of high quality, and an exceptional network of contacts with the world of management and technical expertise. Consequently the first aim must be to replace today's monopolistic, hierarchical, and selective model with one that is more open so that no institution can escape competition. Competition has also to be brought to bear on the results accomplished, not on the selection of students and the rank of the institution in the selection system. To accomplish this, these institutions must be rearranged and structured entirely differently. In France, as long as each institution remains limited to only one set of specialties in which it predominates, it is inevitable that the result of tradition will keep it in the rank in the hierarchy that it has always had. To overhaul this system, these small, narrow schools must be merged into more diversified universities that would cover all of the main specialties. This regrouping, or rather reconstruction, would allow three or four institutions to maintain a fairly equal competitive relationship. Nothing but good could come from such an attempt at despecialization because scientific and technical developments tend to produce new tasks and new disciplines that supersede old specializations.

The effort that is required to merge and rebuild ancient institutions, which are jealous of their autonomy and based on extremely powerful alumni associations, may seem too great to be worth the attempt. It is an undertaking so foreign to our habits that it threatens to scandalize many people. It is not just a question of the quality of our elite but of our whole society's capacity to innovate. We are always talking about industrial redeployment. Can this happen without intellectual redeployment? In a world where the capacity for scientific knowledge, imagination, and experimentation is more and more important, it seems of prime importance to develop our most precious resources of this kind. There is a palpable contrast between our boldness in business and our timidity regarding educational institutions. The government and bureaucracy put immense efforts into rebuilding whole sectors of industry, where large-scale mergers are either suggested or required. These interventions concern enterprises over which the government has no legal control, whereas the elite training schools are totally dependent on it financially and have only a small degree of legal autonomy. This area is decisive for our future and is one of the few in which there is no practical obstacle to action by public powers. That alone should be enough to make it a top priority area of action.

Are the necessary rearrangements really so difficult? It is fairly easy to see a natural clustering around the most substantial institutional leaders. In the areas of technology and science, these are the Central School of Engineering, the Paris School of Mines, and the Polytechnic School. In administration, management, communications, economics and social science, they are the School of Advanced Commercial Studies, Business School and Research Study Centers, the Institute of Political Science, and National School of Administration[2]. In addition, these two areas should be opened up to one another since technological universities devote a large part of their activity to management, and simultaneously management schools are developing real competence in highly technical specialties such as data processing.

This institutional rearrangement would eliminate the hierarchy among schools and would allow some stimulating competition to develop. But to open up the French elite, the number of people admitted to the schools must be allowed to increase. It is an inescapable law that narrowly based elites will always act in a Malthusian fashion, whereas more widely based elites, goaded by internal competition, will tend to be open and willing to change. Of course, precautions must be taken. Too great or too rapid an enlargement would lead to the creation of an elite core within a group that was too broad. In this, as in many other cases, growth is not positive unless it is based on a balanced development of human and institutional capacities. Rearrangement, the identification of new goals, and a totally different analysis of students' career opportunities can make healthy growth possible, which would lead to double or triple the number of students admitted to these institutions.

It might be objected that it would be better to devote all of our efforts, and our monies, to the development of universities, which already deal with a broader population. I do not think so. The elite training schools exist, and it is possible to change them but not to eliminate them. So long as they exist, it would be inconceivable to raise the universities to their level. Reforms can prepare the ground for some of them to achieve this gradually, but it would be disastrous to move too quickly. Here again it is important to be very certain about our aim. What we are after is improving the French elite system, not giving the best university education to all who seek it. I will come back to the problems of the university in the next chapter, but I want to emphasize now that it is important to have examples to go by and to try new things level by level. Today's elite training schools are capital that must not be wasted. Their rearrangement and development would be a difficult operation, to be carried out with the greatest care, but it has every chance of success. Such a success would have important consequences not only for the direction taken by the elite but also for the development of knowledge, research, and the university world in general.

One last problem remains: the selection process. These new institutions, even though enlarged, would remain of high quality. How are students to be chosen for admission? The qualifying examinations today are the focal point around which the French elite is structured and which make up the foundation and legitimacy of the hierarchy. A person who has passed a qualifying examination is already located in a social hierarchy, no matter what he does afterward. Therefore it is essential that the qualifying examinations be transformed. An open system can never be established as long as this principle of selection dominates all the other areas of activity of the elite schools. I think that it would be best to keep the classes that prepare students for the examinations but to change the classes fundamentally. For example, they should be absorbed by the new institutions and have as their aim not the selection of the best but the elimination of those who cannot keep up with intensive instruction at such a high level. This would simplify the problem because it would no longer be a question of classifying as rigorously as possible applicants who are to be steered in one direction or another because of slight differences. It would be a question of keeping a large majority of students, already selected according to their qualifications at the beginning, on the basis of their performance in examinations during the first two years of training. The years at preparatory schools have been called barbarous, outdated, and sterile. It is clear that there must be a substantial broadening of both the content and the methods used in teaching. This is why these classes must be directly integrated into the institutions for which they prepare people so that their practices can be reworked according to the needs they fulfill. But at the beginning at least, the teaching framework they represent should not be allowed to collapse, and continuity has to be ensured.

The elimination of hierarchical selection upon entry is not enough, however. We must deal also with the range of choices at graduation, which forces students to take internships only for prestige. Why should the top ten students in the graduating class of the Polytechnic School start their careers in the administration of mines, and the next forty or fifty in that of bridges and highways? The elimination of this kind of classification would pose no organizational or teaching problem, and it would have a great effect on the spirit of the institution and on the behavior of students. It is crucial to develop other reasons for working besides the aim of scholastic success. Students are much more sensitive to the interest of knowledge for its own sake than is often realized, particularly if it is linked to independent study and can permit them to make an original contribution. Some people say we already have enough researchers and that research takes people away from practical life and undermines a sense of responsibility. This view of intellectual and moral apprenticeship strikes me as ridiculous. Of course, if brilliant young people without experience are steered into basic research too soon, as is done today, this can lead to scientific sterility and social irresponsibility. But future members of the elite, at a time when they are most receptive, would be allowed to have the experience of empirical work, where they learn to test their imagination and be humble in the search for solutions. Experiments in other countries, and even some in France, show the enormous potential of creative energy of young people between the ages of twenty and thirty.

The system as it stands today takes ridiculous pains to steer young people away from any original contribution. It restricts them to the struggle for class standing, which is much less instructive than the analysis of real problems to which applied research would lead them. And the advanced training programs should be integrated into the new institutions, where they would constitute an advanced program of study. Only a minority of the students would get a doctorate in this program, but all would do their two years of specialized study in it, through applied research that would involve fieldwork and the presentation of research reports. This would encourage a large number of students to work on their own personal scientific contributions. This is the basic requirement for a lively center of intellectual activity. This is how institutions such as California Institute of Technology, Massachusetts Institute of Technology, and the Zurich Polytechnicum earned their reputations. I am not aware that their teaching methods turned their students away from practical responsibilities. This investment in applied research, part of it in basic research, would also have the advantage of employing faculty full time, which is essential for the development of rich and living institutions.

The Reform of the Administrative and Technical Corps

The French elite is only partly an administrative elite. The training schools provide leaders for many other activities as well, and fortunately there are members of social elites who are able to move up by other routes. If this is so, then why base a strategy for opening up the elite on the civil service? Because even though the top administrative and technical corps are not the only center of the French elite, they are certainly the anchor of its hierarchical system and the source of its legitimacy. It is impossible to be successful in reforming the elite schools without transforming the elite corps at the same time. Together they reinforce one another perfectly and for the most part are run from the top. As long as there is a hierarchy of technical and administrative corps, there will be an irresistible pressure to keep or restore the present structure.

Let us look at the system that the mining engineers constitute today. It includes three hundred people divided into three approximately equal sectors among the administration proper, the nationalized sector, and the private sector. For the most part, administrative posts are occupied by young people. They stay there ten years and then move on to jobs in the private or nationalized sector. Then they bestow the same promotions on their colleagues from the Polytechnic School, who are promoted less frequently to these positions. The typical hierarchy is as follows: The presidents or top executives coming from the mining engineers, then department or division heads who are from the Polytechnic School, and then engineers who are plant managers and bureau heads from less prestigious schools. Only a minority of French industries follows this pattern exactly, but it is a minority that counts: the whole nationalized sector, except for Renault, most large companies in heavy industry such as steel, nonferrous metals, chemicals, electricity, nuclear energy, and banks and insurance, the last of which is almost entirely under the control of the Office of Finance. The leaders who are chosen in this way generally are of high quality, but this model of organization tends to reproduce the defects of the administrative bureaucracy. These include a stifling centralization, an oversupply of executives, the irresponsibility of officials, the weight of overregulated organizations, and a lack of adaptability and imagination.

How can this be remedied? I see no solution other than the gradual elimination of the top administrative corps. This is the only way to cut the umbilical cord between the administrative system and the business world, to rid young people of the illusion of royal careers, and to make the elite system richer and more alive. Such a break has to be risked because the elements of a new order exist already. Big businesses do not depend on the existence of the top administrative corps. Although they do recruit some of its people, this is because they need people who can deal effectively with the bureaucracy of the state. It is not necessary for the top executives of the French industrial world to get their first experience in public administration. And there is no technical requirement, no particular ability, no pressing need that justifies the existence of the top administrative corps. Of course, there are the examples of the Council of State and the State Audit Offiice, which need specialized jurists. In order to retain their juridical independence, they have to have a special status and thus be a corps. But it is not necessary that these corps be composed of a super elite, recruited upon graduation from a school that is already elitist and that monopolizes the hiring for top public positions. The Council of State should always seek to recruit the best jurists and the best experts in the areas that concern it. But it is not desirable that the general specialty of a jurist for the Council of State or the Office of Finance Inspectors be thought of as superior to all others. The corps are Malthusian, they are attached to the way of thinking that their power is based on, and they are an insuperable obstacle to the introduction of new specialties required by the management of an increasingly complex social fabric.

The elimination of the top administrative corps, therefore, would not be as problematic, on the level of functions and tasks, as might be thought. But it does pose some problems of internal management, organization, development, and policy. Elimination of the present system of managing the administrative apparatus is unthinkable without our being able to formulate and enact a different one. What should be the basis for this new system? Essentially it should be based on the organization of a true market of expertise. What the top administrative corps are supposed to supply is expertise, and they do it badly. They have a monopoly and prohibit any competition. If this monopoly is made to disappear, competition has to be organized because in this kind of area, it cannot operate successfully without being regulated. First, the nature of this expertise has to be understood much better because it is very diverse. Much of it is internal in nature because it consists of being familiar with the practices worked out by the civil service and with their logic. Another consists of knowledge and experience of a more general nature, such as economics, finance, industrial markets, technological expertise, and management. The rest consists of indirect knowledge because real experts have no access to the civil service. It is essential that in the future new specialties necessary for good management of society be widely accepted without harmful discrimination. In terms of quality and usefulness, a knowledge of public opinion, social and cultural trends, organizational analysis, and systems analysis is as important as financial or juridical analysis. The areas of health, urbanism, and cultural affairs require at least as much attention and care as finance or education. Of course, internal administrative expertise should be retained, but its role should be much more limited and should make much more use of experienced practitioners in this respect. As for specialties corresponding to the principal traditional disciplines, such as finance, law, and economics, they should be revitalized by calling outside help.

For all of these reasons, it seems to me that the French civil service system needs one or two small organizations, similar to the Planning Commission, which would have an advisory role regarding organization and management and which could take care of the technical aspects of regulating this marketplace of experts that has to be created. Japan and Sweden have organizations of this kind. Judicial regulation, for instance, could be carried out by a public administration commission, with a separate status, which could play a much more active role with regard to the rules of competition, such as opening up positions, terms of contracts, and the possibility of changing functions. The jobs themselves, in my estimation, should become contractual. Taking the idea of expertise to its logical conclusion (which also could include the idea of organizing), it is clear that there is a contradiction between the job of a consultant or organizer and the status of a public official. The official expert will always have a tendency to become stale in his routine, thanks to the exclusive control that the existence of his job sets up. Tomorrow's state service will require much more open competition, which can be guaranteed only by hiring experts on a contractual basis. Moreover, there is no reason why these experts should not, after a certain period of service (five or ten years, for example), be able to apply for permanent employment positions in which they would give up their role as consultants. Finally, the consulting jobs must be filled by people from different backgrounds who do not have experience in administration alone. The last essential element of this reform would be the creation of personnel and organization departments in all large administrative bodies. They would have to be much less administrative and legal than those of today and would be able to play a very active role in the analysis of needs, searching for the available personnel, and in the selection of people.

This reform would be impossible unless it is accompanied by a reform of the elite training schools. Real marketplaces of talent could grow out of these new institutions. The experience of doing research would do a great deal to develop the students. True, the difficulties would be great, but it is a task that can be accomplished insofar as the reform of the elite schools is successful. At the beginning, no more officials of the top administrative corps would be hired, and they would be replaced by consultants. Once there were enough consultants available, the regulation of the market in expertise could be set up, and the full-scale reform of top public officialdom would be finally underway.

A Strategy of Building Institutions

In closing, I would like to come back to the overall strategy addressed by the reform I have proposed. I have talked of a strategy of breaking up institutions. This is only a partial description. A strategy of creating institutions must be discussed as well, and perhaps above all. By this I mean investments in people, methods, systems of organization, and thought rather than in buildings. By this I also mean an undertaking that is durable and of high quality. I am not talking of destroying what exists but of investing this capital better and in different ways so that it will produce more dividends. To pursue this capitalist metaphor a little further, reforms should use human resources, which we are now saving without interest, in such a way as to use the best market for investment that can be imagined today: knowledge, expertise, and intellectual capital. This capital certainly does include the acquaintances, the relations, and the prestige of the elite schools and the top corps, and it particularly includes the immense potential energy of young and talented people, who today are being wasted.

The objection might be raised that the elimination of the top administrative corps is not a job of creating an institution but quite the opposite. This makes sense only in the narrow logic of ritual form. The top administrative corps are self-serving institutions, little interested in promoting innovation, and their place could very well be taken both by new academic creations of international standing that could be created from the elite schools we have now and also by the networks or markets of consultants that I have suggested be created. Finally, the partial and intended imbalance introduced by such a reform could be the starting point of the new form of political regulation that I said was both indispensable and impossible. It means breaking things up and making provision for imbalance but guided by the immediate possibility of creating an institution, with the aim of creating future institutions.

The possibility of this breakup and its beneficial nature rests, however, on a gamble, one that gives priority to knowledge to fight technocracy.

7
AGAINST TECHNOCRACY: THE STRATEGY OF KNOWLEDGE

Knowledge as a Value in Development

Knowledge is frightening. People respect intelligence and talent but not knowledge because knowledge implies the risk of change. It confronts people without concern for their wants or what they believe are their needs. It throws the established intellectual and social world into turmoil. True, it promises development and growth but it is primarily a test of reality. This leads to the ambivalence about it that is felt both by the man in the street and by leaders. We all know that the benefits that are expected to result from discovery and material progress will have a cultural and social cost. All development of knowledge involves risk because it leads to change whose direction we cannot control, even though it takes place through and with us. And the behavior of a society in the face of knowledge is of decisive importance. A society that is capable of accepting the risk involved in knowledge will evolve, while a society that avoids it will decline.

As in all modern societies, and perhaps more than in any other, French society fosters this contradiction. Science is good as long as it is disembodied. But technology, which is dangerous and inhuman, is subject to the worst kind of manipulation. Hence the thinker has a noble and pure image, but the technocrat an arrogant and hateful one. Our elites and leaders are of two minds. They know that science makes and commands the future and are therefore ready to invest in it. But the fear of being threatened remains. They want tangible and risk-free results. Investments are made in programs, not in people. They try to govern science rather than support open scientific communities. This leads to a policy that is narrow and too ambitious. It is made up of brief moments of enthusiasm that arbitrarily disrupt routine, followed by long periods of somnolence and the short-run practice of giving in to the pressure of interest groups who have succeeded in making up the scientific establishment. But no reform of French society or of any other society can succeed without relying on the basic value that knowledge represents for humanity. It must not be seen as valuable for finding the truth but valuable for change or, in other words, for its usefulness. Science answers metaphysical speculation with the possibility of action. It cannot take the place of revealed truth, either in its bastardized Marxist version or in its most rigorous positivist forms.[1]

Any strategy for change has to give priority to knowledge. Consequently it has to work so that scientific and technical communities will be open and vigorous, so that there will be more rapid and lively communication among basic research, the application of knowledge, and its final utilization, and so that society will be ready to run the risks that knowledge entails. Every government is duty bound to make citizens aware of what is involved. Its role is not so much to make good choices in scientific development as to make society able to take risks and make these choices itself. For this, the problems of the scientific and technical community, the carriers of new knowledge, have to be taken as seriously as are the fears of Frenchmen about the risks of change inherent in this knowledge. The two problems are related, and their solutions are not necessarily contradictory. The fears of the public are understandable, but they are directed the wrong way. The power of technicians does not result from the progress of science but rather from its blockages and misdirections. The way to make scientific development more effective and diminish the danger of technocratic takeover is to open up the world of knowledge.

The fact is that we do not seem to control anything anymore. Experts are everywhere, imposing limits, making people recognize their limitations, determining the right options. All-important decisions are made by different technicians, who have no consideration for what people are going through. Some people think that eventually computers will be able to make all the decisions without us.

But reality is quite different. In the first place, computers have never decided and never will decide anything. Specialists do interfere, and many people in positions of responsibility do hide behind the computer to impose their own decisions. But this behavior is nothing new. Experts have always imposed their solutions, and people in power have concealed their wishes and desires behind the decisions of experts. The blacksmiths of the Iron Age, the architects of the days of the pharaohs, and the bridge builders of the late Middle Ages all had much more influence than do the computer experts of today. And if the social sciences did not exist, astrology would take their place. Of course, the fact that the problem has always existed does not mean that we should stop fighting it. But the experience of the past can help us to do this more effectively. The competitive interactions of knowledge, not regulation and the halting of development, are what eliminated the technocratic brotherhoods of the past. The increase in the number of experts and specialties made it more and more difficult for a small group to monopolize an area of activity. The power of the technicians is on the rise again today, it is true, and a new technocracy is more frightening than one that people have succeeded in bringing to heel. But what is important is not to ascertain whether the situation is worse today; it is to be able to control and transform it.

The paradox is that the more demands for protection against

new things that are made—that is, against knowledge—the greater the chances of increasing the power of the technocrats, who do not benefit from the free play of knowledge but from uncertainty and restrictions. If knowledge were apparent to all, technocracy would be impossible. Useful programs are those that organize human relations in such a way as to prevent the monopoly of knowledge, not by an individual, which has become impossible, but by a group. Groups must be opened up, knowledge demystified, and deeper knowledge used against false or half-true knowledge. The technocrats are most dangerous in the least precise and least scientific areas, such as marketing, education, and health.

Moreover, the power of the technicians is essentially conservative. They become involved in development only after inventors and real innovators have been there first. The technicians often wait for an innovation to succeed abroad, or, what is worse, they make up an artificial specialty that prevents the problem from being directly attacked. This is the case in France with many public decisions, about which it is more important to know the administrative procedure than to have a real understanding of the problem.

In the end, the easy way is to regulate, guide, and attempt to direct the development of knowledge because people prefer today's chains to the risks of tomorrow's freedom. Unfortunately this leads to giving more favor to knowledge inherited from the past at the expense of new knowledge. The present is not allowed to be enriched with the fertilizer of the future, and in the end it is easier for knowledge to be monopolized by the same establishment that was to have been muzzled. To adopt the strategy of knowledge, openness, and change requires much more effort and courage. But it means casting one's lot with the future, working to safeguard the capacity of a society to play a role in the evolution of the human race.

The problem is crucial for a country like France, whose material resources are fairly limited and which cannot keep up its economic activity—and finally cannot continue to exist—unless it aims for a much more sophisticated course of development based on knowledge. Such a gamble can succeed. There is a substantial capital consisting of tradition, know-how, and values. But intervention is essential because our system for producing and distributing knowledge is falling apart. If we do not manage to reverse this trend, we will not easily be able to adapt to the modern world.

Reactivating the Research System

The first problem to be dealt with is research and the social system that carries it out. Without question, knowledge is developed only through official, specialized research. The value of a separation between amateurs and professionals might be questionable, but in developed societies the core, the training capacity, and nearly all of the effort of basic research is carried out in specialized institutions. To deal with the problem of the production and distribution of knowledge, the research system has to be understood beforehand. I insist on using the term *system* because institutions generally are thought of only anecdotally or in a strictly utilitarian way, in the interests of programs or individual people. It is too easily believed that good choices of programs or people are enough to obtain good results. But research does not just consist of immediate results. Its development over time changes problems themselves, as well as the ideas people have of problems and their results. It is also a human creation, which may or may not be one that is concerned with individuals. Good research is not done by good programs but by good researchers. Good researchers are not made simply by making the selection process more difficult but by encouraging them by the existence of an active, lively, and aggressive scientific community, a better research system.

The research system includes the selection and training of people (universities and elite training schools); the production of knowledge (laboratories and university institutes, elite schools and the National Scientific Research Center, private laboratories); the distribution of knowledge, a market or series of markets dealing in people, programs, and finances; and finally one or several scientific research communities, with their standards and networks of influence. This system is extremely complex because of the number of its elements and also because of their interdependence and interpenetration. Businesses depend on the educational system and on the job market because they need their help to recruit their specialists and executives. But there is no symbiosis between these institutions and business. It is different with research, in which the universities are simultaneously institutions of teaching and knowledge production. Each of these closely integrated subsystems has extremely different cycles of effects and reaction times. Selection and training and the distribution of knowledge all have long-term effects, whereas financing has short-term effects. Certain subsystems have international frames of reference, such as the market and scientific community, and others do not, such as scientific institutes. There is a tendency, particularly in France, to see only one side of a problem, the narrow, instrumental one. Attention is given to the relation between financing and results without realizing the systematic effects that make for its efficiency.[2] Ignorance of these effects is disastrous. It explains the succession of infatuation and disillusionment that has been the hallmark of the history of research in many countries, including that of France.

This picture may look bleak. There is certainly some light in all this shadow, but the overall outline shows very restrictive mechanisms. The opinions of the two French Nobel Prize winners in the recent past, Monod and Guillemin, are the same and clear on this point: French research is dying of bureaucratization. It is appalling that their recommendations, in spite of being widely read, were totally ignored by the authorities. The system is closed, not because French researchers are culturally resistant to contacts but because bureaucratic procedures set up a high wall between the National Scientific Research Center which includes most full-time researchers, and the universities, and because even higher walls are built between industry and the National Scientific Research Center and between the universities and industry. The attachment of professional researchers to the National Scientific Research Center tends to disparage the part-time researchers at universities and the less "noble" researchers in industry. Doctoral students, who in many countries are the most highly motivated and aggressive work force in research, are often neglected, and amateurs are excluded entirely.

The closed, monopolistic character of the research system is the result of its being a state organization. French researchers are not satisfied, even though they are well protected and unlike their foreign counterparts enjoy a very generous security, and in some respects total independence. On the contrary, they suffer from the weight of bureaucratic rules governing their institutions and even more from a total lack of mobility. There is no marketplace for talent in French research. Because of this, there is limited competition among institutions, and governance of the whole can be carried out only through the use of centralized, bureaucratic control mechanisms. These are hardly effective at correcting the self-protective behavior of the notables of the community. This system leads to compartmentalization and even to fragmentation. No one has much interest in cooperating with anyone else. Every institution is jealous of its autonomy and seeks to get the most it can at the expense of its competitors. In

the weakest disciplines or areas, the result is a ridiculous fragmentation. In sectors that are strong or have existed for a long
time, the system is built around traditional poles of activity. The
danger is one of conservatism because the most promising areas
are often new ones, which span different disciplines and cut
across jurisdictional and institutional boundaries. Finally, the
strategy of research suffers from the conditions of financing,
which leave no freedom of management to those in charge and
which oblige them to juggle their budgets in order to keep their
institutions operating.

Now let us look at the major institutions that carry out most of
the research. The National Scientific Research Center is a very cumbersome institution, comprising some ten thousand researchers. It is subject to limitations of personnel and budget. It was
created to escape the paralysis of the university but has become
paralyzed itself. The conversion of its employees into government
officials (which is not required by law but is happening anyway)
is the principal cause of this, along with the immense size of the
institution and its inability to avoid centralization. The high rate
of growth it underwent in the 1960s gave it a certain dynamism
for ten years. But the crisis of 1968 and the present freeze on
hiring are beginning to have devastating effects. The conservative
reaction of the unions to this recession has had the practical effect
of preventing young people from having access to jobs in research, which means elimination of all sources of internal
dynamism. A simple demographic projection shows that if this
policy is continued in a discipline such as sociology, in ten years
94 percent of the researchers will be more than forty years old.
This is an extreme example, but the same trend is at work in all
disciplines. What is more, the universities are not suited to take
up the slack. They have difficulty cooperating with the National
Scientific Research Center because of problems regarding legal
status. The fact that there are cases of combining functions ar-

ranged by many notables in the field should not deceive us. The institutions only rarely work together. And the research laboratories of the big industrial concerns also live in their ghettoes. Contacts take place only on an individual basis and generally only at the highest level. The first agreement negotiated between Rhone-Poulenc and a public biology laboratory stirred up a storm.

The government is vaguely aware of this ponderousness and paralysis and has tried to take action by starting priority programs, coordinated actions, and contractual programs. The General Delegation for Scientific and Technical Research has been its main working tool, but it too became quickly paralyzed because the weight of administrative factors in making scientific choices became too great. The strictness of the management of programs always seems more important than their content. In any case, despite appearances, nobody is really interested in human development and in the important problem of the dynamism of institutions. Personal problems are never dealt with except from the point of view of legal protection. Pressures from unions and bureaucracy combine to make the management of personnel completely separate from the problems posed by the labor market and even from the accomplishment of the task. That nearly all the research staffs have tenure is a serious problem, and will be disastrous in the future unless something is done about it. The problem may appear to be minor from the point of view of budgets and the number of people involved, but it is crucial for the development of French society. It is urgent and essential that this be dealt with quickly.

Despite appearances, choices regarding the research system are much more important than reforming the taxation or even the educational system. By concentrating resources, the research system can be revitalized fairly rapidly and, thanks to its contributions, human resources and useful ideas can be available elsewhere. But what is to be done? Three major problems must be dealt with: the mobility of researchers, the institutions and the place of young people.

How can the mobility of researchers be ensured? Of course, everyone is in favor of it, but the restrictions that need to be lifted are such that this remains a pious hope. But is it acceptable that research be a life-long career even though for most people scientific creativity does not last more than ten or fifteen years? A group of life-long researchers cannot help but become a group of officials seeking to defend technocratic privileges.[3] The effects of this are not apparent at present because large-scale recruitment took place fairly recently, but they will be felt very quickly and very strongly. This group's power of resistance is substantial, given the advantages that researchers enjoy, particularly their remarkable independence. For changing the pattern, mobility must be made to pay, which means that attractive opportunities must be opened up. Three converging avenues can lead to this, in my opinion: setting up an internal job market between universities and research organizations, systematic canvassing for opportunities in industry and civil service, and the gradual conversion of researchers into contractual consultants.

Because researchers enjoy job security, it would be fruitless to try to go back on this pledge. On the other hand, it seems legitimate to make contractual the period of time spent doing full-time research at the National Scientific Research Council or the National Institute of Health and Medical Research. This period of time could consist of four-year contracts that could be renewed, depending on discipline and the project, one, two, or three times. Permanent positions, as in universities, would be awarded only in exceptional circumstances, in the light of results obtained, or for the precise functions of laboratory directors or of large research teams. The positions that were freed this way could be offered to university personnel who would finally be able to do some research and effectively retrain themselves. Researchers leaving the National Scientific Research Center would have to accept teaching positions left vacant by the professors. Promotions in both cases could be subject to performance. This internal mobility alone would obviously not increase job opportunities, but it would multiply each person's experience, restore the quality of the university, give life to the whole system, and get people used to change. It is to be hoped that some new opportunities would develop along with the new ideas.

Creating new jobs means going much further. Why not use this method to organize exchanges between the National Scientific Research Center and industry, between the National Scientific Research Council and the civil service? Industry researchers and consultants of the civil service's research staffs would greatly benefit from the experience of more basic research. The interaction of basic researchers with another profession could also be fruitful. It would lessen the chasm that exists today and would lead to the discovery of new possibilities. This would not eliminate the active search for jobs, but it would help it. Institutions of management, which are now crushed beneath their heavy and useless bureaucratic burden, should give most of their effort to the job market as part of an active policy of disseminating information. Management functions should be returned to operational laboratories and institutions. Any moderately rigorous analysis shows that abandoning many of the conditions and supposed controls would in fact decrease waste. Conversely a lot of effort should be given to the development of these operational institutions—to find out their best size, depending on their disciplines, problems, rhythm of development, the quality and training of their personnel, and the strategy of their research. It is heartbreaking to see that at present bureaucratic restrictions are the only structure for the most sophisticated system there is: the production of knowledge.

The problem of young people is perhaps even more important because in this regard the young are our most precious resource. To deprive them of access to jobs in research, as protective pressures are doing today, means laying the groundwork for a disaster for French science. According to today's conditions, not many positions can be opened up for the young. Even if more opportunities were opened up, some of them would be taken up by exchanges and the development of the system. Nor does it seem realistic to increase the number of research positions immediately. There are too many financial limitations, and the expansion of the 1960s could not be repeated without running some risk. A larger body of researchers would create great confusion and would make for even more insoluble human problems in the future. Therefore the numbers should be increased only insofar as their weight has a reasonable chance of being borne by the whole social system. This seems possible but only if serious thought is given to the importance of the contribution that research makes. Perhaps the extra effort for research should not be borne by an expansion of positions and burdensome programs but by the human investment of doctoral research carried out under decent scientific conditions. Research institutions might be given the basic task of organizing this doctoral research as part of their own programs. Many programs would be less expensive if they were carried out in this way. The pressure of developing research would be much less inflationary, and the responsibility of laboratory directors or research staff directors to find jobs for their young people would lead to the acceptance of research work as an educational discipline more easily than a bureaucratic employment office could do.

For this system to be set up, universities and elite training schools would have to agree that programs for doctoral research be organized by or with research institutions. Right now, this requirement would arouse a lot of resistance, but its desirability is obvious. The reform of the elite training schools could certainly lead to its acceptance. But in any case the present way of doing things has to be dismantled.

Reforming the System for Using Knowledge

It is not enough to reform the system for producing knowledge. It is essential to deal with the system for using it at the same time, not because balance or logical coherence are desirable but because the demand from the outside world is a force for renewal that must be used. If the system for making use of knowledge remains conservative and cautious, the reforms of the research system will be stifled. Of course, the production of knowledge is a driving force in itself, but it cannot overcome certain obstacles. Moreover, a powerful demand for knowledge can be a source of pressure, a fundamental lever, for the success of a reform of the system that produces it.

However, it should be made clear that the production of knowledge should not be subject to social demand. Besides there really is no clearly visible, socially created demand. There is rather a bilateral relationship in which the supply of knowledge creates a demand, while the utilization of knowledge, because of the problems it poses, stimulates its production. The multiplicity of experience and viewpoint that this relationship stimulates is a favorable breeding ground for the development of knowledge that is also the product of a social network. To develop it, it would be foolish to try to impose programs on it, even when they are useful. The social relationships that support it must be enriched. Upon examination, the quality of the existing relationships can be seen to be much more complex and much less neutral than is often thought, and they are extremely diverse in texture as well as in quality. In some cases there is a relatively open market in people and knowledge, but in many others isolation and fragmentation are the rule. The users of knowledge quarrel over possible monopolies, and researchers barricade themselves behind their expertise and refuse to recognize those involved in practical matters. The social fabric is weak and tied up in vicious circles. Knowledge is poorly distributed. Nobody is able to see the true perspective of a situation because many data, as well as real lessons of experiments already carried out, are partially or entirely concealed.

To develop and enrich this social fabric, an indispensable task for the success of the research effort, what is most important is to be familiar with practical matters in order to put pressure on the sensitive points of important subsystems and to have realistic chances of changing their regulations. In this regard, even more than the others, we have to work according to the specifics of the situation. General formulas, uniform rules, and impersonal bureaucratic management, which are the habitual recourse in France for finding solutions acceptable to everyone, have disastrous and absurd results. True, we must invest and reform everywhere, but this does not mean that our actions must be uniform or even that the principles have to be the same. The strategies adopted could be entirely the opposite, depending on the characteristics of the markets and the system of research, their complexity, their maturity, and particularly the nature of the various scientific disciplines involved. Certain systems, such as those of the social sciences, require a strong effort at transforming the system for disseminating knowledge. For others, the existing knowledge market can be relied on. For still others, it has to be created from the ground up. The problem of renewing the system for making use of knowledge arises in different industrial sectors, not just advanced technology industries. It arises particularly in areas of rapid innovation such as communications and services. But in each case the problem is different and must be studied in its own right.

However, there is a key area that has to be considered first, that of public decision making. Curiously here the use of knowledge is even less well understood than in industry. This is a crucial area for society, where great progress could be made. And this could be designated as a leading area of action because the possibilities for mobilization and organization are great and the chances of success are fairly good. But the existing situation is deplorable. We have a remarkable corps of administrators, our politicians have ability, and real or supposed experts abound. But public decisions are very poorly made, worse than fifty or a hundred years ago. They are subject to the internal needs of the administrative machinery and the interaction of recognized pressure groups far more than by a logical consideration of the facts. Our leaders have ideas, many ideas, but a poor knowledge of the facts. Nobody seems to understand that no realistic strategy can be worked out simply on the basis of ideas, however brilliant these may be. Nobody will admit that it is simply fashion that guides these ideas rather than the real dynamics of the society.

Let us take the extreme example of the over-centralized French educational system. Ideas for reform are innumerable but, unfortunately, contradictory. From time to time, though, an idea becomes a fad and changes are made. Given the centralization of the French civil service, these changes are the result of public decisions that are subject to long debate. Now, these decisions are never based on serious analysis. People argue on the basis of facts that they do not know, or rather on the basis of norms and principles, with implicit hypotheses about the behavior of the people involved. These hypotheses are totally baseless, and the results are not related to what was intended. This immense body of 800,000 people, one of the largest centralized organizations in the entire world, has no research bureau that is worthy of the name. Its research institute, the National Institute for Pedagogical Research, works in its own ghetto, in as academic a way as possible. At present, there is no one who can say how a French school works, what the problems of its administrative staff, teachers, and students are, far less what the deep, implicit rules of operation of the system are today. True, there are authorized persons who speak in the name of each level, but are they talking about reality? In any case, nobody speaks for the total body of the scholastic community. Officials "know" how things work because they made up the official rules and because these rules are enforced. There are difficulties, of course, but they know about them. As for why things work the way they do, everyone has his own idea, with his plan for improvement on definitive reform. None of the highly delicate decisions that centralization requires—in the areas of scholastic organization, teaching methods, participation, or content of the programs—makes any sense unless it is based on a fairly serious analysis of the facts. And people are not in a position to know them.

The examples in other areas are perhaps less dramatic, but they are countless and just as clear. Bureaucracies provide a lot of information about what they do, but the data they work with correspond only imperfectly to reality. Let us take the example of a bureaucracy that is big but very well run and that undertakes a gradual but general process of computerization of its main activities. This transformation will change radically the duties and functions in its main occupational categories of personnel. The installations have already aroused some entirely foreseeable reactions, which were treated kindly, but nobody thought to take advantage in time of the lesson this provided. The directors are thinking of the problem of computerization and change in an abstract way. Eventually they will touch on the problem of adapting their model of organization in terms of their limitations but without having made the initial attempt to understand the human reality of the personnel and executives. Everyone keeps on thinking in terms of rules of advancement and legal status, whereas the real question is how to define the responsibilities of practical organization of operations and to choose the objectives to pursue on the human as well as the material level.

I have noted our ignorance concerning the diffusion of knowledge. The same is true for the human background of industrial markets. It would be useful to have dependable data in order to work out an industrial policy. Is it not possible that our successive failures and the practical impossibility, about which we have been quarreling for fifteen years, of going beyond brilliant ideas and syntheses is due mainly to this lack of respect for the facts? The dramatic crisis in the French steel industry is the most distressing demonstration of this.[4]

Another example, among many others, is that of social services. It is clearly absurd to have committed the considerable expenses that we devote to the various areas of social service without a clearer knowledge of the reactions of the public involved. What errors could be avoided if we could analyze in advance all the data about a problem, if we could bring ourselves to do a few experiments, especially since we are capable of doing this. Much progress has been made on this in the last ten years. Large-scale, precise surveys that make it possible to understand people's real behavior are becoming commonplace in other countries. Experimentation with social services, which was considered unthinkable, was carried out with far fewer problems than expected. In the United States, excellent information has been accumulated, even if the complexity of the federal decision-making system has made it impossible up to now to use it.[5] The policy of aid to education, expenditures on health, and aid to cities will also be deeply affected. In France, we are fascinated by computers and dream about data banks without realizing that the data are more important than the banks and the facts more important than the computers.

Most important is the lack of capacity for analysis at the top because the difficulty lies not only in the absence of data but is particularly a question of how people think. Only the location of teams of analysts next to those in power can lead to a different way of looking at problems. According to the present state of thinking, administrative and technical expertise monopolize the field. Problems can be looked at only through the filter that they use to guard against any political interference. Political interests are not thereby totally eliminated but are reduced to their narrowest range of expression, that of the demands of interest groups. It is urgent that another type of knowledge be used to break out of the vicious circle of blunt, categorical demands and blind bureaucracy. I am not talking about prior knowledge that is ready to be applied but of knowledge to be created and recreated. Only the method for learning it can be taught.

All relevant problems for working out a real strategy must be presented and then followed by systematic analyses on which studies, large-scale surveys, and experimental programs can be based. Strategic proposals must be worked out as a function of these analyses and the cycle of "means-data-problems" must be constantly reconsidered. The state of existing means for action and their effective use must be analyzed. And finally the initial analyses must be extended and gradually differentiated in their specific application to involve more local people in the discussion. Direct command will then gradually be replaced by cooperation based on a unified method and agreement on the facts. The contradictions inherent in the real world will not be escaped, of course, but more effective solutions to them can be found, and learning processes can be started to allow these contradictions to be overcome. In order to solve the problems I have pointed out—industrial policy, educational policy, regional decentralization, elite training schools, research—these research staffs have to be relied on. The same is true for health policy, employment policy, and that of social services and population. The only way to make progress is to change the nature of the problems, by injecting new ways of thinking and knowledge and by forcing leaders to be aware both of the true effects of present practices and of the alternate possibilities that exist.

These research staffs conceivably could be tried for coordinating offices such as Planning or the Budget. But they can be successful only if similar staffs are quickly established in the offices of operational executives, first at the highest level and then gradually going down the hierarchy. The expense may be frightening, but it would be much less than it may appear and would very quickly return a profit. These staffs should not number more than a few people, and their existence would make it possible to do without many hierarchical relations and useless controls. Gradually people would be taught to use more and more large-scale methods, like the big surveys and experimental programs tried in other societies. These far more costly methods should be used cautiously, but would be extremely profitable from the point of view of society as a whole. Why not spend the few million francs needed to avoid the waste of hundreds of millions that every major administrative action produces?

It might be surprising that I suggest the general establishment of these research staffs at the main operational levels. This distribution seems necessary as long as we have to fight the separation between thought and action that paralyzes political and administrative decision-making. The new ways of thinking at the top will be effective only if they are also internalized at operational levels, which should therefore have information and a substantial freedom of thought. Moreover to go from direct command to a more flexible governance, it is necessary to develop tools of thought that people will have in common, and the increase in the number of research staffs is the best way to succeed in this. Some may fear that this invasion of experts may make the bureaucracy even more ponderous and limit the freedom of officials or, worse, of citizens. I think, though, that the existence of these research staffs would make discussions clearer and would bring to light the reality that the bureaucracy conceals. Surveys give citizens a much better voice than any intermediary can. Can there be any more democratic step than bringing a better knowledge of the facts into public debate? Surveys, analyses, and experiments are, in the end, the best defense against the omnipotence of officialdom.

Relying on People

In the sixteenth-century, Jean Bodin, a Frenchman and one of the first European economists, said that people are the only wealth. It is time to return to this piece of wisdom. People make their future and make themselves, not programs or doctrines or structures. However, paradoxically, a huge collective effort is necessary for them to succeed. This is where institutions have an irreplaceable role because they are the social fabric in which each person can find and form himself, which means creating his own freedom. If this fabric is weak, institutions are restrictive and human freedom is weak. If the network of institutions is active, on the other hand, they can be less restrictive and can foster freedom and progress. These assertions may seem commonplace, inspired by an outdated brand of humanism. But their value is not philosophical. They are judgments about the progress of human social systems, whose purpose is to be the basis of a strategy.

Knowledge plays such a large role in our society today because it is becoming the new determining factor in the social fabric, for two reasons. It requires the development of new activities and functions, which leads to differentiation of roles and greater complexity of institutions and the possibility of change in the social fabric. Above all, it can be applied to this social fabric itself and make better management of our social activities possible. In France, this possibility is not well understood, if only because of a panicky fear of manipulation. Using a strategy of knowledge does not mean fearing manipulation; it means relying on people. Rather than trying to protect them at any price, it means refusing to prejudge for them what they want to build. This trust in people can be ridiculed, but I do not see what it can be replaced with. How can we be so arrogant as to refuse to grant the ability to choose to those who follow us and who have greater knowledge because of our efforts? The most basic purpose of a strategy should be to leave a freer future for the generations to come.

This is the trust in people that I am suggesting when I talk of creating institutions. It is implicit, for example, in the priority given to the reform of the elite training schools over the universities, because reforms with a future are chosen over reforms that are logical. When the movement that values knowledge has enough momentum, the universities will follow of their own accord. The real risk is not one of failure but of society's becoming a closed system. Of course, even if important reforms succeed, it is quite possible or even probable that the new system in turn will show a tendency to become closed. Even elites that are more numerous, more intellectually open, and more efficient can certainly hang onto their privileges and, on the pretext of maintaining quality, succeed in blocking the system again. But this should not stop us. Is it not better to struggle to create a more open system today and leave the task of continuing the job to our successors?

By now it should be clear that this strategy for change gives an important role to individual and social learning. The future is not blocked, and we can become freer because we can learn new ways of behaving. Knowledge is of value for the future because learning is possible. Our method of teaching still thinks of learning as the communication of a preestablished body of knowledge, but it must be changed to experience in the real world. What is missing in our educational system—at the primary, secondary, and university levels—is teaching people to make choices. Relying on people implies that they are capable of making choices, which is a trust implicit in any democratic ethic, but also that they be allowed to learn how to make them. People learn to make choices by testing their tastes and abilities and in gradually discovering the variety of possible experiences. French adolescents are particularly at a disadvantage in this regard because of the heavy restrictions that the secondary school ladder places on them. In order to keep as many options as possible open to them, they have to refuse to try what they would like to and must even do what they dislike.[6] The system chooses where the individual should be. Relying on people means building new schools where the freedom and responsibility of adolescents would be much greater.

8
FACTS AND FANCIES

Putting Aside the Pressures of the Moment

Many leftist readers will have been convinced by some of my analyses and suggestions, but then will have said that my thoughts, however interesting, could only really serve as a useful complement to traditional structural reforms. It is doubtless good to think of all the possible ways of eliminating the bureaucracy and to prove the technocrats wrong. But, they will have said, these are only secondary operations to be added, given the time and the means, to the great projects of eliminating inequality, reforming business, nationalizing monopolies, and giving workers' management of industry.

Naturally I am not ready to accept this position. The strategy I have begun to develop cannot be considered by any means as a complementary strategy. My top priority is to reverse the trend of bureaucratic organization, the decision-making style in public and private affairs, to open up the elite and transform its way of thinking. However pressing they may seem, the matters presented by thè Left, as well as those presented by the Right, do not seem to me to be truly urgent. They are perhaps worthwhile objectives, but a logical strategy cannot be built around them. Far be it from me to defend today's inequalities or to defend traditional authority. I think that our society has too much inequality, which should be reduced as much as possible. At the same time, the transformation of our pattern of authority is unquestionably the basic problem of social change. But I do not think that a strategy with any chance of success can be based on these value choices.

Equality and democracy cannot be obtained by decree any more than virtue can. They are won, earned, or gradually built, to use other metaphors. Despite appearances, this argument is not specious. Whatever definition is given to the principle of equality, it cannot be imposed as such on a population. To succeed, it would be necessary to eliminate any possible way for anyone to discover how to use the advantages he has to change his situation. To do this—as every regime that gives priority to equality is led to do—another form of inequality is introduced, one that separates the controllers from those who are controlled, the simple citizens and the bureaucrats. Manipulations of ideology and emotion can succeed in covering up the problem, but in fact they will only make it worse. The same is true for authority; authority cannot be made to disappear by authoritarian means.

In the years before 1978 the socialists claimed that the priorities of the Common Program of the Left were of another nature. So did the English Laborites, the Social Democrats, and the most liberal partisans of welfare in the United States. I do not believe this for a moment, and in order to explain my opinion I would like to try to develop the major themes of the struggle for change as they have been argued over the last few years.

The Illusions of the Struggle against Inequality

The struggle against inequality was the main mobilizing message of the Left during the 1970s, which was all the more powerful because the Right did not dare oppose it.[1] The contrast with French society before 1968 is striking because then much greater inequalities were accepted with remarkable tranquillity. In reality, this morally tinged theme has played such a strong role in our collective consciousness because it has served to express a deeper social and existential malaise.

All evil is therefore supposed to come from the scandalously unjust distribution of incomes, capital, and even power. Any measures, actions, and reforms that attack this serious problem are supposed to be valid. Otherwise reformers are accused of refusing to make structural reforms. In this regard, the remarkable theory has even been advanced that inflation itself is the result of inequality. It is true that Holland and Sweden, which are the most egalitarian countries in the world, have until now suffered less from inflation than most others have. But the fact that countries with a lot of inequality have little inflation as well, such as France in the 1960s and the United States, does not seem to bother the people who think this way. Nor does the fact, based on experience, that periods of rapid redistribution of income go hand in hand with periods of very powerful inflationary pressure.

The struggle against inequality had become the key to a strategic choice, by which it was hoped that we could steer toward a harmonious society that would allow new economic growth. It is this choice that I criticize, not the fact that we must struggle against inequality.

Yes, ours is a profoundly unequal society, and we must speed up the progress to equality. But we have to find effective means for action. Salaries and incomes cannot be fixed by decree. Prohibitions and limitations can have an effect, but these are always temporary and do not mean very much. And so the argument about the maldistribution of incomes seems to me to be highly theoretical. There are an infinite number of ways of escaping the law, and the more the system pressures wage earners, who are the only people who can really be controlled, the more the speculative sector profits from it. The lavish income from black or gray markets in socialist countries is testimony to this. The only effective means of action against inequality are the classic ones used by Sweden and Holland: direct taxation, the progressive tax on inheritances (which is much more profitable than a tax on capital in this regard), the guaranteed annual minimum wage, and the even wider development of social coverage. Unfortunately these methods are not easy to institute in France because of certain aspects of our administrative system, our social system, and our customs. Reformers are paralyzed by the mysteries of our taxation system, which is the product of our administrative and political traditions and of the social equilibrium of a society that for so long was rural.[2] Every increase in taxes produced violent reactions. Even the "drought tax" to help farmers, which affected only higher salaries, seemed shockingly arbitrary.[3] Locked into this system, we have neither the human resources nor the intellectual capacity to reform it.

To make any progress, an agency for intervention has to be created, one for which knowledge is fundamental. The publication of the first serious analyses of incomes in France, a result of the work of the Center for the Study of Incomes and Costs, should be praised as a tremendous step forward.[4] But aside from the exact knowledge of material facts, decisively important psychological and sociological problems are totally neglected. If these problems are so obscure, to the extent that data now being discovered risk being quickly forgotten, this is because obscurity is a natural defense mechanism of society. The French adapt well to the obscurity that results from administrative complexity because their position is ambiguous and because, behind their dreams of fraternity and equality, they are extremely fond of all inequality, particularly its more petty forms. In fact, the problem is much more complicated than it seems because differences, advantages, rewards, and stratification are all forms of protection that individuals continue to need. It is not possible to suppress them without suggesting something else.

So among other things we found in a now-dated study of the

employees of a large nationalized bank, the clerical workers are fairly satisfied with their work and their situation, at least as satisfied as junior executives.[5] We naively believed that this finding would be seen as a "good finding," and in fact this is how it appeared to the directors of the bank. Then we got permission to show these results to union representatives and small groups of junior executives. To our astonishment, this went very badly. We showed the same figures to twenty groups of ten junior executives. Twenty times, in the same way, the twenty groups of junior executives objected, became angry, and expressed resentment. How could their inferiors be as satisfied as they were? To them, it was terribly unjust. Because they were "superior," they should be more satisfied!

Here is another recent example. In an analysis of the attitude and behavior of the employees of several Parisian insurance companies, we had the opportunity to study the reactions of the employees of a company that had made enormous efforts at rearranging jobs and making work more rewarding. The employees work in independent groups in which they have more initiative and responsibility, and two-thirds of the executive levels were removed, greatly simplifying the workings of the administrative machinery. The system worked well from the technical point of view and seemed to be at least as efficient as the previous one. However, even though the employees seemed to be satisfied with their work, they were more unhappy than ever on the whole. Why? Basically because the bureaucratization and elimination of inequalities also eliminated their chances of advancement, promotions, and many privileges. These examples are not unique. The pressure to keep and increase social inequality is still dominant in France. Besides, only in the last thirty years have the complex hierarchies of public administration taken form, which differentiate between no fewer than eleven corps within the Ministry of Bridges and Highways. Private businesses have had to adopt a system of stratification, with its classification matrixes, which they did not have before.

So it should not be surprising that in in-depth interviews carried out yearly by a French research and marketing institute to follow the change in attitudes and behavior of the French, the theme of equality does not come through strongly. Much stronger are those of freedom and the autonomy of the individual, impatience with authority, freedom of expression, and the development and affirmation of the self.[6] A wise government should not let itself be led by the obsessions of the political and intellectual world. France has never been a country of workers except in very small part. Now it is becoming a country of petty bourgeois, who are passionately attached to the distinctions, privileges, and subtle differentiations of a hierarchical society that in many ways are out of date. This is so even of those who vote Communist; real proletarians hardly vote at all. Of course, this system can be thought of as absurd, inefficient, and morally sterile. But this condemnation should not be made without some understanding because human beings cannot live without some protective devices and prejudices. We have to try to make this society improve, not trample all over it.

Public authority has a prime responsibility that is extremely difficult to fulfill: the arbitration between various occupational groups in negotiations for salaries. To a small extent it can exercise its influence in this matter to lead to a narrowing of the range of incomes, and it is already trying to do this. But it cannot go beyond certain limits. It would be a serious mistake to think that any government can effectively give priority to this aim at the expense of social peace and the fight against inflation. There are limitations on doing this through contract negotiations, and prohibitions and the establishment of matrixes and pay schedules are counterproductive. The only strategy that can serve as a basis for fighting against inequality remains an indirect one. By this, I

mean transforming decision-making systems, developing understanding of the facts and the means for action, and identifying
relevant modes of regulation that can control the effects of inequality. Besides there is no general system of inequality. From
this point of view, France is a particularly fragmented country.
Before seeking to eliminate the subsystems, we have to understand all of them within which inequality is created and maintained. There are many unearned incomes to be eliminated,
connections to be cleaned up, and sectors set to rights. This is all
the more reason for understanding them well rather than denouncing them wholesale.

The Game of Slicing Up the Pie

The struggle against inequality is the noble side of the debate
about society; the struggle for the redistribution of incomes is the
sordid side. Here every ruse is acceptable and confusion is particularly prized. Beautiful statements against inequality and in-
justice are often nothing but smoke screens, whose purpose is to
conceal the selfish and dogged attempts of every class to increase
its relative and absolute advantages. The problem is much more
difficult than is often believed. Experience shows that the list of
arguments that can be presented to justify an acquired advantage
is inexhaustible. In fact, everyone is more or less consciously
fighting to prevent the imposition of clear and universally recognized criteria that will permit the definition of a just reward. The
truth has to be faced squarely: everyone wants to retain the
greatest possible freedom to press for gain from the situation he is
in.

There are rules, however, that limit the possibilities of blackmail by the different parties and that allow for intervention

by the state. The social game that is going on is not limited to a direct struggle for a bigger slice of the pie in which anything goes. It is a complex game in which indirect maneuvers, which create a climate in which crisis will develop, may be more important than the phases of the struggle itself. Keeping things obscure is a particularly useful precaution that sometimes makes it possible for the pressures exerted to be covered up, sometimes to make some disclosures more dramatic. It is possible to be indignant about freedom that to a great extent is the freedom to do harm, but in practice it is not possible to separate the good effects from the bad. This is the same freedom that will permit the realization of experience and real change, the adaptation to change, the discovery of different solutions and more positive arrangements. The formalism of the rules can be criticized and also the Byzantine social game that results. Other, noncoercive means should be found for giving expression to the parties involved. The game of slicing up the pie is difficult and puts all players in a morally difficult situation. But it is possible to improve it by introducing more clarity and by forcing monopolies and private preserves to open up.

Here again, we find the value of systems analysis as an instrument of change. Every system of industrial relations or collective bargaining is a fairly autonomous whole that has to be worked on to get results. Clarity, awareness, and action for change become possible as soon as a good systems analysis demonstrates both the facts and the complex relations between and among them. Let me try to say this in more concrete terms. Here is a typical example of the problems of public administration and the major nationalized industries. The female employees of a large business (five thousand people) work very hard under difficult conditions. They often have to work overtime, and their pay is comparatively low. They accept this situation because as women living in the provinces, they have no other opportunities to work in a public agency and do not want to give up their job security. These employees are represented by powerful union federations, which group together many types of workers scattered in very different types of business. The case of the company I studied is very well known, and the scandalous situation was denounced publicly. All the same, in negotiations the union leaders tried to take it as representative of the great hardship of all of the employees of the administration in question. The management replied by pointing to the equally exemplary case of the workers in another establishment who, thanks to commercial and technical circumstances, have the advantage of a fairly light work load and who occasionally abuse it. From both sides, the employees of the first company are the victims of the system of collective negotiation used in public administration and of the mode of union organization associated with it. Everything proceeds as if it were impossible to deal with the real-life setting and organization. These women are pawns, or poker chips, in a much larger system. Many injustices and inequalities of this sort become focal points of frustration and contribute to maintaining an unpleasant social atmosphere. Of course, there are other sources of discontent, which are part of a more general feeling of inequality and particularly of feelings of abandonment and humiliation. And the fact that the decision-making system is frequently and sometimes totally out of touch with the reality experienced by the people involved is a basic source of disruption in social relations.

Let us now follow the game of slicing up the pie at a higher level, that of large-scale industrial negotiations. Here the role of the state is very important, not so much because of its commands, which are seldom obeyed, as because of the straitjacket of rules of representation in which it has succeeded in confining the participants. This does not prevent the opponents, particularly the unions, from often crudely exerting pressure. But they also have to take public opinion into account. The employees of the French Electricity Authority, for instance, were victims of it even before they were ever beneficiaries of it. This leads to a very complex game made up of calculated slowdowns, evasions, and lateness on the one hand, and dramatic accelerations and confrontations on the other. In the general confusion, each party thinks he will get the most out of the situation: the state, which holds the line on inflation no matter what; management officials who retain enough freedom of action to counterbalance their concessions to the unions; and the unions, who always win some advantages and maintain the combativeness of their troops.

But this system is only the lesser evil because it has many inconveniences. It is an anarchic situation in which anybody can stir up trouble. If the circumstances are right, a small, well-placed group can make the state tremble if it is very determined. But once the disturbance is over, the Byzantine system starts up all over again. Rarely are there wildcat strikes in France. In a sense, all strikes are wildcat strikes that are finally subjected to procedures and regulations. Collective bargaining in France is characterized essentially by the fact that no one ever directly discusses the issue. The discussion breaks up by regions, branches, and categories. The general confusion that results is good for all kinds of quiet arrangements that permit the parties to come to an agreement without really being involved and permit the intermediaries—factory and department managers, local union leaders—to maintain their influence. It is a cumbersome and sloppy system, whose results cannot be predicted. The wage drift can be substantial, but leaders—particularly state officials—always keep a margin for action and think they will be able to control them. Anyway, this kind of temporizing appears to be the only way for leaders to slow the deadly inflationary spiral of incomes. From meeting to meeting throughout the year, the state officials manage to tire out and exhaust the beast. And by choosing the right moment, they have opportunities to point out the extravagant nature of some of the demands.

Evidently this system is very difficult to change because it, like the bureaucratic system, is protected by its weight and confusion. An aggressive strategy for change cannot be based on it, in my opinion. But it is essential to try to make it change in order to use it to bring about a less unequal distribution of incomes. I think that the only weapons the reformer has are clarity, which is imposed gradually by the development of understanding, and the establishment of rules of the game that are simpler and more accessible to the mass of people and to public opinion.

Another sort of action should be considered, it seems. Social interaction, particularly the game of slicing up the pie, seems to be dominated increasingly by abstract categories. Executives, employees, specialized workers, low-paid groups all exist more in statistical terms than in common experience, not to mention common will. The abstract solidarity that results from these classifications makes it very difficult to understand what the experience of the people involved is and what is the real nature of their problems. It is impossible to satisfy all of their demands because these are considerably inflated by the contradictory pressures and demands that propel the organizations that represent them. Of course, there is no question of attacking solidarity as such, as this can be important. But it would be crucial for other, more concrete and human solidarities to take their place partially. Union solidarity by company should be encouraged rather than the solidarity by craft or by occupational category. So should the professional and regional solidarities. These efforts are essential to improving societal interaction, as well as balancing and making it healthy without regulation or direct state intervention.

Self-Management: A Mobilizing Idea or a Fantasy?

Let us now consider the deepest and most burning issue in European countries: the demand for worker self-management. For millions of young and not-so-young people, self-management has become a mobilizing idea that is supposed to cure all the ills of our organized and restrictive society. Can this tremendous aspiration be ignored at the very moment when everyone recognizes that French businesses are poorly organized? It can. Even though I recognize the deep and beneficial role that the idea of self-management has had in the cultural progress of the country, I think that once carried over into the union movement and the political game, it becomes a fantasy, which serves no purpose but to revive the eternal socialist dream of the virtuous society. It is true that these two aspects are closely intertwined, and the social and, especially, the cultural movement that feeds this fantasy model is a real one that must be considered.

In the last twenty-five years, the climate has profoundly changed. In the 1950s it was almost impossible to make Frenchmen talk about the internal organization of business or any other institution without becoming the laughing stock of the Marxists or the technocrats. It was believed that the collective takeover of the means of production, or free enterprise of the American type, would be enough to settle all arguments. But now self-management has become a basic and widespread demand. Management and human relations, as well as the explosion of May 1968, cultivated ground that until then had not been fertile. But the intellectual genesis of this fashion is not important. After all, self-management was a strong part of the great anarchist dream of the late nineteenth century. It preceded and accompanied the Russian revolution, from the Scottish shop stewards to the *Betriebsräte* of the Weimar Republic, to the soviets, the original principle of socialism (now forgotten) in the Soviet

Union. What is important is the concrete character, power and widespread nature of the return to it. We have no way of measuring it, but the indications are in agreement. The French people in the 1970s had only the vaguest idea of what self-management might mean. Most of them only pay lip service to this myth anyway. But the prevailing values everywhere are those of autonomy and hostility to all authority. Everyone wants to do and must do his own thing, to use the American expression.

I have already referred to findings that show a stronger and stronger trend toward the values of autonomy, self-expression, and self-realization at the expense of values of order, authority, and equality. It is possible to ask how long this trend will last and what real effect it will have on our society, but its existence and importance cannot be denied. What does it mean? Often we are led to make mistakes by a simplistic mode of thinking, which makes us conclude that the power of a social or cultural movement and its future growth must lead to the success of theories that are formulated to express it. In fact, the relation between thought and action is nowhere near this close. Often theories are nothing but an occasional reflection of changes in practice. This seems to me to be the case with self-management in France. There is a movement there, one that is vague, diffused, and very strong, one that involves everyone to some extent. This is what leads to the relative success of intellectual theories about self-management, which in turn rebound and partially influence it. But the two phenomena must be studied separately.

The great weakness of the intellectual movement lies in its coherence and vigor. It is based on a single idea, and any idea taken to the extreme becomes crazy. The complexity of human life, particularly social life, cannot be overcome by a single idea. In this case, human relations cannot be regulated simply by the autonomous organization of the workers. As soon as the indispensable interdependence between people and groups is recognized, some other principles of government have to be sought out: first, the reality principle, which implies respect for efficiency, moderation, and the truth of observations; second, respect for the freedom of others, or the acceptance of their initiatives; and finally, the recognition of the value of development, which implies acceptance of the future, the acceptance of innovation. Of course, all that can be theoretically reintegrated into a more elaborate model of self-management, but it would be impossible to apply without an impossibly cumbersome legal machinery or, as is the case in Yugoslavia, without the constant intervention of an all-powerful authority.

The cultural movement against authority, on the other hand, cannot be judged as if it claimed to be coherent. But the problem it presents is one of its own limits. To live and let live is not enough of a philosophy for living in a world that is too complex. It is very nice for everyone to want to "do his own thing," but fifty million Frenchmen do not live alone, each on his own deserted island. The movement against authority is strong as long as the patterns of authority are real obstacles. But insofar as these patterns are altered and even renewed, I think that a reversal of the trend will be inevitable. After exalting the struggle of the individual against society and institutions, the problem of limits and necessary protections naturally arises again because the response of the free individual is anxiety when confronted with decisions, involvement, and responsibility. It is too easy to blame society for existential discontent, as many young rebels still do. But the movement must slow down and start to reverse. Self-management tendencies, as they have developed up to now, are caught in a deep contradiction. On the cultural side, they express a rejection of authority, of manipulation, and of limitations; this is their benevolent side, in which they show imagination and enthusiasm. But on the political side they solve problems by totally avoiding reality. In fact, for most partisans of self-management, this means a better format to be achieved by socialism, getting rid of the "bad guys" or threatening them, while being quite aware that this is incompatible with the cultural side.

This is perhaps a good time to offer limited but practical opportunities for experimentation to those who wish to express themselves, to work and create in a freer way. From this point of view, we must have a new way of thinking. We must not delude ourselves into thinking that we can thus move from a petty bourgeois bureaucratic society to a communal or convivial society through enthusiasm or constraint. The partisans of self-management have to overcome their distaste and learn that the petty bourgeois and the bureaucrats have virtues that they need. The taste for authority is not the only foundation of our society, and self-actualization is by no means accomplished only at the expense of subordinates. It also is an attempt at accomplishment, expression, and the desire to improve oneself. The only way to make the petty bourgeois and petty bourgeois society change is to have respect for them. But the ultimate demand for the abolition of all hierarchy gradually leads to a bureaucratic growth to which the French Left (and the American Left, by the same token) would have brought us dangerously close. Here is a decisive choice between a difficult though fairly modest effort to open up and take over, in a framework of freedom, and the great hope of a universal solution, which would necessarily lead to a rebirth of constraint and, finally, of authority.

For me, the choice is already made. We must keep fighting for the success of new experiments; it is essential that as many innovations as possible be tried in this area. I will come back to this in my last two chapters. But the most pressing matter is to act on as many breaking points as possible, the bureaucratic focuses of French society, not the establishment of a model of worker self-management.

The Absurdity of the French Style of Nationalization

There is something absurd in the French Left's plan for nationalization because, despite appearances, it is in such deep contradiction to the Left's aspirations and theoretical objectives. The nationalizations, as they were conceived by the Common Program of the Left, could neither ensure the equalization of incomes nor enact a real industrial policy, and they ran the risk of setting up an insuperable barrier to self-management. These assertions may seem arbitrary, so let us look at the facts.

The struggle against inequality is not waged through nationalizations. The countries whose economies are nationalized are not more egalitarian in practice than others. The most progressive countries in terms of the redistribution of incomes do not nationalize their industries. The Swedes and the Dutch, the most egalitarian peoples of the industrial world, in terms of income and political power, who are a hundred times more advanced than the Russians or the Poles, seek to make capitalist enterprise profitable, not to replace it with a state bureaucracy that is more rigid and less efficient. They think, and history has proven them right, that free enterprise—even that of multinational corporations—in a free market is the only system that can ensure a surplus large enough to permit the development of social equality. It is possible to question the limits that this sort of policy should be subject to, and particularly how fast the leveling should take place, but there is no question about the means. The lessons of the experiments being carried out next door to us are perfectly clear—the positive experiences of Sweden, Holland, and even Germany, as well as the counter examples of Poland, Czechoslovakia, and, to a lesser degree, England. In the context of France, nationalizations would have led to an even more painful game of slicing up the pie. New rigidities and the irresistible pressure of the unions unquestionably would have led to an acceleration of inflation and, in a relatively short period of time, to a lowering of the standard of living.

Regarding industrial policy, the problem at first does not seem to be so obvious. It seems reasonable to think that nationalizations are the only efficient means of controlling the economy. The Socialist party assured us authoritatively that without nationalizations, industrial redevelopment cannot be well managed and the economy cannot be run efficiently to the benefit of the greatest number of people. To enact the efficient development of planning, the power of the banking apparatus and the big industrial groups would have to be under control because until now they had steered the economy exclusively for the sake of their private interests. This type of argument is seductive in its logic, but it is the argument of a technocrat or one of the lunatics who say,"All you have to do is . . ." Experience shows that it is much more difficult than is commonly thought to work out a good industrial policy. The best experts, Western and Eastern, have failed. Remember that until the present crisis, the planning system of the steel industry was the pride and joy of the French planners. And even the theoretically best policy would be impossible to apply because economic life, like life itself, defies simple logic. As I have already tried to show, there is no single market that can be controlled but several complex and interdependent markets that can neither be separated nor controlled together. Businesses are not abstract and transparent entities but human creations that are complex, that grow and decline for reasons other than the simplistic economics of Marxists or classical liberals. However able they may be, officials are not capable of thinking according to the subtle logic that is the only useful kind in this area. The obligation to plan, to use the words of de Gaulle, may be very useful when it seeks to act on this logic. But it quickly becomes a cumbersome, inadequate, and backward strategy when it wants to take the place of this logic. Nationalization would only make a bureaucratic industrial decision-making process even more unwieldy and would threaten to become irreversible.

There are two particular factors in addition to these general ones. First is the financial factor. Whatever the type of compensation, nationalizations would involve a cost to society, which is already a problem, but at the same time would particularly increase the capital available for speculative sectors. Like many other Western countries, France already suffers from a disequilibrium between a productive sector that is not very profitable and speculative sectors that are. The latter must be put to rights, and the best way to do this is to reduce their share in the nation's economic activity. Nationalizations would run counter to this pressing need. Second is a social factor. The management of businesses would be made particularly difficult by the risk of a general social crisis that would accompany a wave of nationalizations. To enact the most basic industrial policy, we need tools of government and tools of moderation. If, through internal weakness, businesses cannot have a strategy, any plan for an industrial policy becomes a snare and a delusion. The liberal economists do not seem to understand this either. They reason as if choices and strategies could be worked out and put into effect without taking into account the capacities of the human agent that takes responsibility for them.[7]

It may not be surprising that I insist on the evil effects of a nationalization policy on the distribution of incomes and industrial redevelopment. But how can I then assert that nationalizations would be an obstacle to the progress of self-management? Because there is a tendency to think that the opponents of self-management are primarily bosses and financial interests. Supposedly, making them toe the line would be the simplest way to move concretely in the direction of self-management—except that a society's development does not take place through military alliances. In fact, the bosses are not the biggest obstacle to progress in this area. The facts seem rather to indicate that the opposite is true. In France, new conditions of work and new formulas of organization cannot be developed in public administration or in nationalized industries but in certain private businesses. It is no accident that Volvo, a private Swedish company, has found imitators among private French companies but none in public corporations. For an autonomous work group to function, most bureaucracy has to be eliminated. How can this be accomplished when the regulations prescribe the existence of fifteen or eighteen levels? It has to be said over and over again that the civil service regulations smother anything that moves, develops, or questions conformity, particularly self-management.

Two recent studies that I directed are very clear on this matter. They dealt with businesses generally considered to be advanced industries from the point of view of the organization of work. In one, the elimination of a half-dozen hierarchical levels made it possible for all operational responsibilities to be transferred to autonomous work groups. Not only have the managers adapted well to this, they seem to find it better. Opposition naturally comes from middle management but also, in more unexpected fashion, from the employees themselves, who remain very ambivalent. In the second company, the practical success of the operation is greatly limited by the opposition of the workers, who complain of having fallen under the control of technicians who are much more competent than they are. The atmosphere got so bad that a wildcat strike broke out and led to a deep crisis in the unions involved. Those who believe, as I do, in the necessity of encouraging workers to take charge of the responsibilities of their work will consider these partial failures as the price that has to be paid in a necessarily long process but particularly as important chances for learning. In a system that has no capacity for leadership and innovation, who can believe that it would not eventually stagnate? Any policy that substantially weakens the capacity of a human organization to govern itself makes innovation more difficult. In this sense the nationalizations of the Common Program of the Left would have gone directly contrary to the development of new conditions, methods, and forms for organizing work.

Some might say that self-management does not mean reformist steps by the management but a coherent model of organization that cannot be judged unless it is applied in its entirety. But sociological analysis does not allow this overly facile thinking. No institutional form can be imposed a priori; initiatives, experiments, and failures are always needed. Of course, other initiatives besides those of well-wishing bosses are desirable and even necessary. But these initiatives will not be set free by smothering the potential for innovation and management that we have now. Quite the contrary.

The basic reason for the success of the idea of nationalization in France was the need for security. Nationalizations are a relatively simple answer to the problem of employment. The main advantage of an employee of a nationalized business is job security, so what could be more natural than for many workers to demand this status? But the root of the question goes far deeper than the traditional demand of workers for security. It really is a classic example of regressive behavior in French society, the atavistic reflex of seeking safety in the state. The French hate the state and the bureaucracy that it inevitably engenders, but as soon as times get hard, they run inside the castle walls. This is the main reason why the choice suggested by the Common Program of the Left was dangerous. In spite of the hopes of the partisans of self-management, it really meant an irresistible throwback to bureaucracy. First, it would have led to an excessive increase in the weight of the administration's burdens and then would have provoked both an English-style inflationary crisis over the distribution of incomes and an Italian-style social crisis over the governance of businesses. The only possible answer to these crises, given the pressing nature of French political and institutional habits, would have been a new reinforcement of the state and, therefore, of the bureaucracy.

Giving Priority to Realism

The popularity of the Common Program of the Left had yet another source, its concrete nature. Ever since the French saw reforms that vanished with the first attempt at enactment, they have been impressed by the seriousness of the matter. Nationalization is a concrete image of a structural reform that might be able to change things. This need for concreteness should never be forgotten in strategic matters, but what the French need more is realism. And I think that it is possible to influence them in this way, even though it is less attractive at first sight. The question is not whether French society should fight against inequality, change the organization of work and eliminate excess profits. That goes without saying. The real problem is not one of intention. It is one of enactment. There is a weakness from which French society suffers perhaps more than do others and against which it is urgent to fight: the propensity to avoid reality.

The strategy of change has to be organized around this need for realism. It must first avoid the dangers of retrogression implied by nationalizations and by any step that imposes allegedly rational formal structures on businesses and on all other institutions. The French must learn to forget the illusions that have enthralled them. People can develop themselves and society can become richer through the construction of human relations that are more open and democratic, not by decreeing self-management or participation.

Moreover, it is impossible to force everyone to take on this job of construction, but it is possible to remove some obstacles that are paralyzing it. It is possible to invest in the development of knowledge to experiment and encourage experimentation everywhere. This is the aim of the strategy of openness that I propose for the management of social organizations, for the opening up of elites, for the development of knowledge. But there is another strategy besides that of openness and realism, a more indirect one of development and experimentation. Prudence and realism are not enough; it is necessary to have an offensive strategy. I think it can lead in two directions: toward a strategy of using the spirit of enterprise against the bourgeois and speculative mentality and toward a strategy of using innovation and new services against routines and the bureaucratic spirit.

9
ENTREPRENEURS VS. RENTIERS

Enterprise, Not Industry

The French do not like industry, ministers and presidents have reiterated for the last twenty years. I am not so sure about this. The technocrats have gotten us to admire huge dams, giant rolling mills, Caravelles, and other marvels of our industrial expertise. And we would be quite ready to be delighted again by the Concorde and the fast-breeder reactor if we could be sure of not risking financial catastrophe with the first and ecological danger with the second. Besides this is not the real problem. Is it not even more stupid to fall in love with an industry than with a rate of growth? Towering furnaces and gigantic steel mills are a dream for underdeveloped countries. It is time that advanced peoples, Americans, Germans, Swiss, and Japanese, pay attention to more serious things. No, the real problem is enterprise. The French do not like enterprises; they are afraid of them. They think, more or less consciously, that businesses are machines for exploiting workers, consumers, and citizens and that they are a conspiracy against honest work. Enterprise is business and business is inseparable from profit, and profit both fascinates and repels them. Above all, to go into business for a Frenchman means to become dependent. Businessmen are feudal lords, their employees serfs who can be made to perform duties at will, and executives are vassals or servants.

They forget that whatever its mistakes, a business is primarily the creation of an entrepreneur, someone who takes matters in hand, who innovates, who does what people do not expect, and who therefore brings something to society. Without innovating entrepreneurs, a society becomes stiff and deteriorates. Moreover, a business is an institution in the sociological sense, the best that people have found so far for cooperating and accomplishing what they could not alone. Of course, it is possible to criticize today's businesses, to wish that they were smaller and more dynamic, and that they eventually be managed by their workers. But no reform, no revival, no reactivation of society is possible in opposition to business or without it. To reawaken society and give it new vigor, above all we must free the entrepreneurial spirit.

Why do the French not like business? Why do they think that profit is shameful but inherited wealth respectable? And why this panicky fear of dependence? To answer these questions, it might be possible to blame political idealism and the association that people perceive among capitalism, the ruling class, and business. But this association did not take place without a deeply rooted reason. The heart of the matter in France lies in the strength of the rentier mentality and the alliance it has renewed with the bureaucracy several times in the course of our society's crises. The monarchy had already chosen the sale of offices, privileges, and rental incomes as its principal instrument of government. Revolutions, wars, and crises were always paid for with a return to this protective pact, which is incompatible with the reward of risk taking.

The dominance of the rentier mentality is paradoxical because it is well known that the French spend their time criticizing the bureaucracy, complaining about controls, and railing against the pestering that prevents them from creating and innovating. But every society is full of contradictions, and this is one of the focuses of our social and collective life. We would like to be able to innovate, but only as long as the rest of the world stays the same. We would like to raise ourselves, but only as long as everyone else stays at the same level. We often fight to establish an income that lets us be free, but we no longer know what to do with this freedom. The rentier mentality has corrupted the French bourgeoisie and has turned it away from the entrepreneurial spirit. This is one of the dramas of our history, even though a great country was built in spite of everything, in the course of centuries of mistakes and illusions. The French bourgeoisie has another characteristic trait that is linked to this: the habit of thinking of a business as if it were a sort of personal plantation. From this point of view, a business is not a creation, a collective endeavor, something beyond the individual, but a possession to be exploited or a social stepping-stone. This view makes it difficult to restore to business its power of attraction, its human value.

Free enterprise will not be revived by bringing back the old France of castles and fine manners; that France cannot develop the future. There is often more entrepreneurial spirit among ex-Trotskyites and ex-Maoists than there is among young bourgeois. What has to be understood is that the entrepreneurial spirit is not linked to a specific social category but represents a pervasive value, the equivalent of the salt of the earth for society, and that everything should be done to make this value accessible to as many people as possible. The entrepreneurial spirit is much more than business in the strict sense of the word, much more than private enterprise, and it is much more important.

Sometimes it is necessary to plan, control, and regulate, but these things mean nothing unless there is first of all a creative effervescence that alone allows the entrepreneurial spirit to exist. And it cannot be commanded from on high. No imposed technocratic formula can ever activate a society. Whatever the intelligence and technical brilliance of the planners, change takes place at the most human level of creativity. The only possibility for more human change for our society is to use the entrepreneurial strategy against the rentier mentality.

Enterprise and Inequality

A reader of *Le Monde*, who is my kin and colleague, might say, What about inequality?[1] What about the scandal of inheritances? And by what right do some people, who have nothing but their birth going for them, command others? My answer to them and to myself is that even though it is right to be indignant, the problem cannot be solved by suppressing it. Virtuous measures have always brought results that are contrary to what was sought. For example, inequality cannot be reduced by blaming business but by making individuals pay. The policy of the French Communist party consists of declaring to the citizenry that the profits of big business are an abomination, and it is absurd. The whole Left, in accepting this proposition wholesale, is acting illogically. For businesses to be able to grow, to invest, they have to make big profits. The reduction of inequalities means taxing incomes and eventually taxing fortunes. If the aim is equality, the bourgeois must be made to pay many taxes and be prevented from enriching themselves by various subterfuges at the expense of their businesses. It cannot be achieved by draining businesses themselves, because only they guarantee decent salaries to workers.

This may seem like simplistic reasoning, but it is not all that simplistic. Why should it be so hard to make people admit this, while fifty years of experience have shown it to be valid? The only countries that have greatly reduced inequalities, Sweden first and then Holland, are the very ones that encouraged their businesses and even the multinational corporations to make the biggest profits possible at the same time as they practiced a drastic policy of income redistribution through taxes. It is not necessary to mention the countries of Eastern Europe; consider simply the case of England. After thirty years of a poorly managed policy of equality, the English have achieved the restoration of inequality in every area of life, along with stagnation and chaos.

France has had a strategy of industry and expansion but in the process has bullied its businesses and tamed its entrepreneurs. Unquestionably we have obtained results that are spectacular in some respects, but the result has been a tremendous cost in inequality and efficiency. If during these fat years businesses had been able to make substantial profits and found it in their interests to invest them rather than divert them in the form of various advantages and privileges, French industry would not be so fragile. In France it is fashionable to blame businessmen, who are supposed to lack imagination and courage. But the ruling bureaucracy has the businessmen it deserves. And considering the qualities demanded of the owner of a company, what bureaucrat or politician has a chance of doing any better?

I would like to go back a bit here. As we have seen, the principal problem of Western society is the deep crisis of our patterns of management, authority, and government in the face of complexity and the explosion of human freedom. Business is one of the main areas where this crisis can be observed. Until now, business has come through better than the governmental bureaucracy and better than the whole political and administrative system because with its dependence on results it has a relatively clear reality principle. But it too is endangered by the bureaucratic phenomenon. The inefficiency of bureaucratic management is outrageous. It is not necessary to mention its frightening results in Eastern Europe, both regarding material production and its human and moral costs. In Western countries as well, the bureaucratic pressure we have given in to for too long is in the process of smothering us. In our changing world, bureaucracy is neither a regulative nor a counterbalancing mechanism but an agent of disintegration or entropy. It is incapable of adapting itself, and it paralyzes innovation, the only action that will allow a society to adapt in an active way. This is so not only of the state bureaucracy but even partly so of the bureaucracy of private business.

The entrepreneurial spirit must not only be revived against the bureaucratic and rentier mentalities in society; this has to be done within businesses themselves. It is no longer acceptable that the best personnel go into positions of control and that they always have the advantage over the functions of innovation. A business is not run with conciliatory words aimed at making a consensus possible. Innovation and enterprise are not carried on with an attitude of compromise but with a strong vision and, if possible, with a strategy. People are convinced by results, not by compromises. Only competition can be the guide and encouragement here. Real consensus comes after the fact and is the sigh of success rather than its precondition. The old joke is well known: What is a camel? A horse designed by a committee. No committee, particularly an all-party committee, has ever succeeded in designing a horse that could run.

Some might say that French businesses work poorly, that they have an outdated notion of authority, that they are basically paternalistic, and so they have to be reformed. True, French businesses need to make an immense effort, but for it to succeed, it has to be clearly understood what a business is, and all steps have to be based on this understanding rather than on axiomatic principles. Reacting against a paternalism we seem unable to get rid of, it is too easy to think in terms of control, countervailing power, and power sharing. This means that we tend to want to prevent, prohibit, and preempt it for one group, only to give it to another. Or rather, in a more moderate way, we think in terms of concentration, participation, consensus, which in the end mean the same. This sort of logic leads more or less rapidly to either a refusal to reform or to a paralysis stemming from the mutually neutralizing possibilities of action on both sides.

For human organizations to be more active, living, and enriching for their members, we need more entrepreneurial spirit, more initiatives by more people. If power is thought of as an asset with a fixed rate of return and that it cannot be given to Paul without taking from Peter, the problem cannot be solved. Progress is possible only because the sum total of power in action in human activities can be extended, mainly because of the explosion of interactions and communications between people. You accept that I have power over you only because I accept your power over me, and we cannot succeed unless our interactions increase. It is not a question of thinking in terms of control over others, of limitations and humiliations. In both senses, countervailing power or the power of control, if taken literally, means paralysis. The real problem to be solved is how to develop initiative and inventiveness. Individuals and groups must always be able to suggest experiments and carry them out. This cannot be done alone, and it is necessary to learn how to do it. There are many obstacles to this sort of development, not to mention the serious problem of middle-level executives. But there is no other solution.

What could be more natural? It is absurd to want to divide power between those who know and those who do not, between a person who has an idea to develop and one who has come to learn. Rather the one who has to learn should be allowed to develop his own idea in turn—or rather, from the point of view of the rational modern business, give back to the small groups the ability to take responsibility more directly for what it can do on its own. This is better than participating in something that is too big or using officious controls to paralyze those who should be working out a strategy for the survival of the whole enterprise.

The sharing of power through workers' control, comanagement, or equal participation is a limited idea and a reactionary one. The development of entrepreneurial spirit and practice is the only way to break the circle of traditional power, the only hope for freedom and fulfillment.

The Problem of Middle Management and the Blanket Effect

How can French businesses recover the entrepreneurial spirit, stimulate initiative, become active again, and start changing? To answer this question, we have to take up our diagnosis and try to understand the operating problems of business today. Permit me to go back for a moment to the crisis of government. The old-time master sergeants have long since vanished, but while clear, personal authority has declined, hierarchical stratification has considerably increased. And while it underwent excessive growth, it became a honeycomb structure in which everyone above a certain level depends on everyone else, in which nobody commands and everyone obeys. This is true in businesses as it is elsewhere. Of course, they are less affected than the civil service and look like models of realism and responsibility in comparison to universities, but they are affected nevertheless. The general public hears only an echo of this through what is called the discontent of middle management. But what are they complaining about? Not about their work, which they claim to love, but about poor and compartmentalized organization, about being cut off from supervising executives. French businesses are not really businesses at all but part bureaucracies in which the routine and rentier mentalities are stronger than the desire to be creative.

The fault does not lie in people, be they executives or workers. French workers are at least as hard working as those in any other European country. Their desire for work is not weakening, in spite of what people say.[2] Of course, there are places where people do eight hours' work in five hours and beat the system at the risk of increasing the number of defective products and of breakdowns, but we are far from the chronic unproductiveness of the English. The resources provided by French workers are much greater than is commonly believed, particularly now that the demand for women workers has been added to that for men. Of course, the French want work that has greater value, and they want to be listened to more. But how can you have one without the other? As for the executives, they certainly are too full of their importance and privileges, but look at their work: what effort, what zeal, what need to achieve and fulfill themselves!

So what is wrong? All of the complaints expressed concern the system's organization, compartmentalization, the difficulty of communication. The sociological diagnosis is identical with the way people generally feel. But let us consider it for a moment, because even though everyone agrees on the problems of business, the remedies they suggest would only make the problem worse, and possibly irreversible. The dominant idea, on the Left and the Right, is that French businesses work poorly because they do not have a consensus and that we must therefore require more group participation (according to those on the Right) or workers' control or self-management (according to various shades of opinion on the Left). Now if sociological analysis is pursued in depth, it is clear that the situation is not so simple and that each of these remedies is strongly contraindicated. In fact, consensus does not necessarily lead to initiative, change, or even productivity. England, which was the typical European country of consensus, is best testimony to that.

What gives vigor to a business is not participation at the top—which always brings out either manipulation or rhetoric—but the chances for taking the initiative at the bottom, or at least at the level of operation. The success of Japanese businesses, for example, is due above all to the extent and strength of their initiatives, the real cause of the consensus that rules there. What French businesses need the most is realism and the spirit of initiative, not participation or control. Everyone who talks about business, be they politicians or even psychologists, are still battering down doors that have been open for a long time, laboring to fight against an authoritarianism that nobody claims or even exercises any more. The scourge of business is not the authoritarianism of ferocious chief executives but what I call the blanket effect: the establishment in the hierarchy of a chain of command, of soft layers of directors, assistant directors, managers, assistant managers, with ranks and functions mixed together, and so interdependent upon one another that nobody knows who is really in charge of what or how decisions are made. This blanket cannot be pierced by those at the top or by those at the bottom. Reorientations, urgent directives, and reforms are lost in this formless mass, and subordinates who would like to improve their efficiency beat against it in vain. All the pious preaching about participation in the future will only make the trouble worse.

This blanket effect is the natural consequence of a very simple sociological mechanism. In a complex institution, where communications are essential but difficult, the intermediary levels get power and profit from this difficulty. Because they are the necessary intermediaries, it is in their interests for communication to be difficult. And often without realizing it, they slow it down and distort it in order to assert their existence or to carry out their job. The problem here is not one of people but the nature of the relationship. This is not a half-baked sociological pronouncement. There is abundant proof of it, as soon as one gets beyond generalities. At the French Electricity Authority, I was able to study a transformation in the relation between installation electricians and district supervisors. The transformation was

successful, but its consequences were immediate: the two intermediary levels, foremen and group managers, who had thereby
lost all of their influence, were deeply unhappy. The example
that I gave of the middle management of a big bank provided the
same lesson. All of the experiments with autonomous work
groups run up against the same problem. The taking of responsibility by production workers allows them to communicate directly with higher levels of authority, who are finally able to
know what is going on, and the lower and middle layers of management are short-circuited. These successive studies over the last
few years have confirmed for us that this mechanism is at work
everywhere. Higher up the hierarchy, relations between levels
are harder to decipher but basically the same.

Under these conditions, imposing consensus and making consultation mandatory means giving vested interests new ways
to block needed reforms. Such a choice would be even more catastrophic because we are on the threshold of far-reaching changes,
partly because of the pressure of production workers for more
consideration and responsibility and mainly because of the new
possibilities resulting from technological progress, computer
technology in particular. These changes are essential and will
make it possible to make better use of production workers and
shorten the chain of command. In this regard, French businesses
are not well off because the chain of command is particularly
cumbersome. Our productive apparatus supports too many managers, just as our economy supports an administrative bureaucracy that is too big. It is not only a problem of cost but first and
foremost one of routine that is the main obstacle to social change.
The middle executives are the people who, as a social group, are
most opposed to the better use of production workers, and to the
clarification of the process of cooperation.

As far as cost is concerned, it is clear that the relatively low
salaries of French workers in comparison to those of certain other

of their European counterparts, particularly the Germans, are directly related to the much heavier burden of executives in French businesses. True, French executives need not be thought of as profiteers living off excessive incomes, as is the case with certain speculative or liberal professions. But the comparison with Germany on this point is striking. The proportion of all salaries in the total value added of industry in both countries is about the same, meaning that the "lower compensation of blue-collar workers' manpower in France in comparison to Germany is due primarily to the existence of greater inequalities within the industrial wage-earning class."[3] White-collar workers in France are relatively more numerous (27 white-collar workers and executives per 100 workers in France compared to 23 in Germany) and they are much better paid (average ratio of 170 to 100 in France compared to 128 to 100 in Germany).[4] This situation can no longer be easily tolerated as it was in the past because we no longer are enjoying economic expansion.

Until now the dominant trend in France has been to diminish authority and, hence, the vulnerability of those in power while maintaining the social hierarchies that protected them from contact. This temporizing policy, which was directed above all toward defending established positions, now has placed us at a disadvantage. From now on our job is to follow the opposite policy: to reduce social hierarchy, to open up as many avenues as possible, to push contacts, and to restore individual responsibility if not authority. For thirty years, the entire intellectual and then social trend has been toward fighting the "myth of the leader." There were strong and good reasons for waging this fight in a country with a military tradition that gave so much value to a dangerous and anachronistic paternalistic ideology. But the myth of the leader disappeared long ago. In a follow-up study twenty years later of the relations between supervisors and subordinates in a group of insurance companies, we found not one supervisor who would define himself as authoritarian, still less as a leader taking command.[5] The ideology of human relations has not been completely internalized by most executives, but human relations have not improved as a result. In fact, we have replaced the myth of the leader with the myth of the group, and if there is any paralyzing and reactionary ideology that has to be destroyed, it is this one because the French-style group, in our institutional context, is the best refuge for indecision, irresponsibility, and hypocrisy. It produces routine and unrealistic attitudes. We need to reaffirm the values of initiative and personal responsibility, to counter vague consensus with the hard lessons of realism and facts.

This means giving priority not to the economic and financial point of view but to the realities actually faced by people and what they bring to a business. From this perspective, French businesses still understand themselves very poorly. Modern methods of management are much less trustworthy than is often believed, and in addition, like ornaments, they are often stuck onto the way things really are. The French business of today has much to do to adapt to the more direct and difficult but also more open and egalitarian world that is in the process of being born. We must help it invest in these changes, and public agencies must invest in collective methods of aid. But let us not impose any more restrictions on it, let us not impose more rules and conservative laws, because these would make it even harder for them to undergo the necessary changes.

Forgetting the Dream of Industrial Democracy

We must go even further. The immediate problem of French businesses is the renewal of their system of control, the revival of their management structure, and the development of better and shorter channels of communication and responsibility. But the underlying problem is the very image and concept of enterprise, where too often there remains the impossible dream of industrial democracy.

Winston Churchill said, "Many forms of government have been tried, and will be tried in this world of sin and woe; no one pretends that democracy is perfect or all wise. Indeed, it has been said that democracy is the worst form of government except all those other forms that have been tried from time to time." (House of Commons, 11 November 1947) I think that this aphorism expresses a profound truth. Without knowing a society's aims and without being able to measure its results, the election of representatives and their democratic control must be accepted as the lesser evil. But discoveries and innovations are never made by votes. The success of an experiment is what gets results. Of course, a business is not only a source of innovation but also an enduring human creation. It has to be controlled and be subject to laws. Unions are a more human and direct means of internal control than are impersonal legal rules, but neither laws nor the power of unions should be able to prevent a business from testing the quality of its innovation on the market. It is not only an economic problem of output but a problem for society as well. If there is no innovation—and innovation can take place only outside the big administrative and judicial machinery—a society can no longer breathe. I am not defending private enterprise here but enterprise itself. If private enterprise remains indispensable, for the moment and perhaps for a long time, this is because no one has succeeded in developing collective forms of enterprise that can keep the capacity for innovation for long.

Some might say that capitalist enterprise exploits workers and corrupts society with consumerism. This is true, but who can do better? In the final analysis, after scores of years of gigantic economic mistakes and the direct oppression of the workers and all citizens, the Russians and the Chinese are obliged to come to study the wonders of Western and Japanese rationality. There is no question that much remains to be done to make our societies more human. But when all the dreams of industrial democracy crumble before the difficulties of experience, people cannot defend as an article of faith the simplistic idea that the best way to run a business would be to give responsibility for it over to workers' soviets. We have enough to do to stimulate, renew, and make our local and national forms of government more human and democratic without wasting our strength on fruitless attempts at imposing an impossible industrial democracy.

Some will accuse me of confusing state socialism with self-management, advanced democracies with backward countries, but I am not. I simply believe that self-management, even in a moderate socialist political and union context, can lead only to state power and that our advanced democracies are backward in relation to the course of human development, which will not stop in 1980 or in the year 2000. The liberation of the citizen and producer requires the maintenance and development of human enterprises, in which creative individuals and groups of people, who have legitimacy because of their own vision and their capacity to take risks, will be able to train and lead others to create new things.

Some maintain that corporations and big industrial empires are doomed in the long run. Personally, I do not think that they will grow any more and may even decline. But in the future enterprise will be even more important than it is today.

What about the alienation of the worker in front of his automatic machine, faced with the assembly line? I have two responses. First, the number of specialized workers is getting smaller and smaller. If we look a bit beyond our national horizon, we can see that the proportion of manual workers in the actively employed population is already down to 23 percent in the United

States, compared to 38 percent in 1960. Some American futurologists think that it could go down to 5 percent in the next thirty years. The massive use of computers will also rapidly reduce the proportion of routine office jobs. The days of union struggles against alienation in the work place will soon be over. What unionized workers are fighting for more and more is to keep their jobs the way they are without regard for monotony. And it is to be hoped that business will succeed in its development and gradually eliminate jobs that are no longer profitable, particularly those whose retention would make essential innovations impossible.

Consider the press, even the French press, today. What could have been more innovative than the radical daily newspaper *Libération*? *Libération* succeeded only because it was a real business, an organization put together by a group of innovators out of which one or two leaders gradually emerged, who are just as much in control as a boss in a medium-sized business. What was the tactic of these innovators? The first to use the most advanced photocomposition technology, they could bypass the printers and their union and put out a daily at a production cost that was low enough for them to do without advertising and without a big capital investment.[6] For years, no capitalist could accomplish such a transformation, though it is inherent in the logic of technological development. The vast technological potential that has built up with scientific development will enable many other innovations like this one. They will be promoted and used by the most varied kinds of people in widely differing ways. We can expect an extremely rich harvest of social experiments.

In this new future, the unions, if they do not change, are in danger of ending up on the side of those who want to keep established rights, which in the end means on the side of the powers that be. Even now some surveys indicate that in public opinion, unions are on a par with the major political parties and businesses as the institutions to be most criticized.[7] True, they will continue to play a useful role. It is good for innovators to have to take time to consider the consequences of what they are promoting. But that role must not be made into something sacred. Above all, the choice of giving unions a role in the governance of a business, or even leadership in the development of self-management within a business, would be catastrophic.

Just as we must free ourselves of the myth of the group in the process of decision making, we must get rid of the myth of industrial democracy in the organization of businesses. Groups are naturally conservative and are productive only under conditions of particular tension and competition. Industrial democracy would combine all of the conditions that allow groups to get bogged down in the logic of inefficiency. Good money chases bad in places other than the money market: the cycle of unemployment and inefficiency is also a vicious circle that leads to crises and, if bankruptcy is unacceptable, to state domination. The conditions required for the maintenance of a fertile tension are much more difficult now than they used to be. Compare the experience of the Lip factory with that of the Albi glass works eighty years ago, which was a successful attempt at workers' management. Look at the dwindling resource the Lip factory has turned into, where the remaining 400 workers of the original 1,200 (of whom none were ever to be let go) now spend the whole day discussing the creation of a cooperative, which will employ only half their number. Such a crushing failure is the most striking symbol of the pitiful dreams of so many do-gooders.

For an Entrepreneurial Policy

The basic problem of French society is not employment, not social peace; it is getting rid of the rentier mentality. If we want to survive, we need a strategy for the future, and that can only be built around the entrepreneurial spirit. But to use the entrepreneurial spirit, people must first understand what enterprise is. Our technocrats have allowed themselves to be confused by a very poor understanding of American economic life. They believed Galbraith when he denounced the technostructure and asserted that it has succeeded in squaring the circle. Thanks to the management of supply and the conditioning of the consumer, indefinite expansion was assured. In the United States, it was worthwhile for a time (but only for a time) to criticize the technostructure strongly. But to take these pretenses at scientific management seriously when a time of tremendous disruptions was beginning was testimony to a singular case of blindness.[8]

The ferociousness of French government in its imposition of mergers and reorganization has not served the entrepreneurial spirit well. It almost brought about some nationalizations that would have been catastrophic, and with a few exceptions (those in which the state did not intervene) none of these mergers was successful. Even if critical mass is an important factor in many markets because of the internationalization of the economy, large businesses need first of all a minimum collective capacity and a decent decision-making system to control themselves and maintain their vitality. After 1970, the McKinsey specialists themselves had warned the French that the positive effects of a merger would not show for an average of ten years, compared to only three in the United States. Subsequent events have not proven them wrong.[9]

Industrial reorganization also has harmful effects. True, it can make people change their habits, and so they change and sometimes innovate. But the most dramatic industrial successes of the postwar years have not been mergers but splits. As Norman Mac-Rae says very well in a remarkable article on the new trends and challenges in business: "The one successful sort of government intervention in industry since the war has been trustbusting by mistake. The foundations for German and Japanese miracles were laid by the victorious allies' 'punitive' action in splitting the old zaibatsus into more and originally smaller groups; they thought they were limiting German industrial power for the future, but were instead increasing it when they broke up I. G. Farben into three smaller and therefore efficient firms."[10] The competitors of IBM hope that the existence of the giant is preserved, because they know that if it were divided into five competitive concerns, they themselves would have a great deal of difficulty in coping with the competition.

There is another basic reason for the deep misunderstanding about the possibilities of the entrepreneurial spirit and the opportunities it holds for the future. This is the close association that has developed among enterprise, money, and capitalism. The entrepreneurial spirit is much more than private capitalist enterprise. And private enterprise itself, under the new technological and financial conditions, can become much less dependent upon capital. The transformation of technology, first of all, can make it possible for businesses to be started with very little capital. I have mentioned an exceptional case in publishing. But the communications world in general may tomorrow offer extraordinary opportunities. In other areas the use of computers and the market distribution of machines that carry out many functions could give back opportunities to the isolated inventor or to the small group. A more open financial situation, in which the availability of capital is greater than the demand for it, may lead to a reversal of the present dependent situation of the innovator. And in the final analysis, I think that French backwardness was much more dangerous as regards the efficient use of what Americans call venture capital, meaning the financing of risks, than the lagging behind of conglomerates and capital concentration.

If we look ahead a bit, we must think of the capacity for survi-

val of these much-talked-about multinational corporations that
are ready to smother a suffering humanity. MacRae asserts, with
very good arguments, that these giant businesses are now on the
decline. Their expansion has reached its limits, and the terms of
political exchange are and will continue to be more unfavorable
to them. They are vulnerable because they are highly visible and
are subject to extortion by all governments. And they will be incapable of keeping their vitality for long because they do not
have the means for maintaining the entrepreneurial spirit alive
inside themselves. Are these speculations or dreams? Remember
that at the most auspicious moment in the great German economic miracle, the masterstroke of the Krupp people who managed to reorganize the giant concern led to the most striking
economic failure of the postwar period. And it is worth noting
that this was a great opportunity for the German steel industry. In
any case, the big industrial groups of tomorrow will be able to survive only under two conditions. First, they will have to be able to
disinvest in time. The society of the future cannot fail to undergo
disruptions that are even more violent than those of today, and
businesses that let themselves get closed in by the simple Gal-
braithian conception of managed demand are sure to remain its
prisoners until they go bankrupt. Second, they have to succeed in
giving birth to new enterprises from within themselves in playing
the role of launching pads for innovators, in choosing to learn
rather than plan.

What policy could be developed from this questioning of many
commonly accepted ideas? It might be concluded that the state
and society itself have little to do. But in a country like France,
the situation is already so strongly oriented in a dangerous direction that an immense effort is necessary simply to allow society to
breathe. An active opening toward business, something totally
different from a policy of financial privileges and abuses, would
be the opposite of giving up. I have neither the means nor the

qualifications to work out its terms and conditions, but I think that three basic orientations have to be kept for the task at hand: the attempt to invest in knowledge, to invest in people, and a strong effort to make it easier to have access to technological and financial potential.

I may have repeated the recommendation that we invest in knowledge a bit too often, but this is because the situation is desperate. It is no longer enough to go ahead with a debunking of commonly accepted ideas; we have to develop an understanding of the human reality of business, of the real activity of markets, of the development of technological, economic, and social opportunities. We complain about the weakness of our businesses the way people used to complain about the shortage of coal, whereas our backwardness is above all an intellectual backwardness.

Investment in people is almost inseparable from investment in knowledge. People who are taught to think and to know the world, who are adapted to the present and future of technical, economic, and social development, are the essential resource for action. To take just one example, instead of complaining about the Japanese invasion that is threatening to ruin our industries, would it not be wiser and more logical to invest in the training of specialists in modern Japanese society? If we compare what is being done in Japanese universities and intellectual centers in the area of French studies with what is being done here in the reverse sense, the superiority of Japan is striking. And this is not unrelated to our commercial relations.

Finally, it will not be possible to ease access to technical and financial opportunities without reliance on a real understanding of the complex systems constituted by markets and scientific and technical organizations. Innovation and public finance cannot be used in the way a financial portfolio is managed or the way legal advantages are impartially distributed. The strategy of innovation requires another sort of thinking.

10
CAPITALIZING ON THE SERVICE REVOLUTION

The Service Revolution is the New Frontier of Business

French society will not survive economically and will not remain socially alive unless it gambles on innovation. In the previous chapter I insisted on enterprise as the active human and social side of innovation. Now I would like to try to reflect on the content of this innovation: enterprise with what, toward what, for what?

It is obvious that innovation above all comes down to individual people. Neither the state nor any public or moral authority can guide them. Nonetheless it is essential to take stock of the areas most favorable for innovation to examine the possibilities that are offered to the innovators. It is a civic duty to fight to force the authorities to make the job easier for them, or at least not to paralyze them. It may sound like naive moralizing to talk like this. But government intervenes everywhere, and experience has shown that it almost always goes against the grain. It is essential that the debate finally be publicly engaged, not about meaningless social choices but about the actual tactics we need to use in order to survive. It seems that a return to realism has already begun in the intellectual world, after the great moral crisis and antisystem hysteria of the years that followed May 1968. In the same year, such diverse thinkers as socialist Jacques Attali, conservative Christian Stoffaes, and Simon Nora and Allan Minc, two liberal technocrats, all tried to find positive answers to the challenges of the new world.

I would not like to take a position on the trends that these authors think that they can discern, so my remarks will not bear on what is threatening to happen but what we must do in light of our resources and limitations, and then I will try to reintroduce the strategic dimension into a debate that too often is purely prospective. My starting point will be the problem of employment, as it is dramatically summed up by Nora and Minc in their report on the computerization of society.[1] The limitations are simple:

1. To keep our place in international competition, it is necessary to improve the productivity of our industries, to ground ourselves solidly in the specialties of advanced technology, and to abandon sectors where we no longer have a chance to become competitive. Because of this fact, industrial employment will hardly increase at all.

2. The traditional service sector of banks, insurance, and administrative services will no longer be able to serve as a substitute for industrial employment, despite what people still think because it will be more and more affected by computerization, which is now inevitable in the greater part of its activities.

3. The only chances for employment that we can find must be sought in the new service sector, in the services involving complex human relations: services to business, communication, education, health, culture, and recreation.

Nora and Minc add, and I am in agreement on this point, that the problem is particularly difficult to resolve in French society, where a smothering centralization impedes the free expression of real needs and paralyzes those who seek to satisfy them.

So it seems that in the future the solution, the new frontier of enterprise, lies in these new services, as long as new technologies will permit their radical transformation. Let use consider again the United States which although it is in no way a model, shows clearly the problems we will have to face. More than half of the population already work on processing information. This fact is shown by a statistical trick, but this classification is no more ridiculous, after all, than the one that distinguishes the secondary from the tertiary sector. In any case, the share of traditional activities—farming, industry, and traditional services—has substantially decreased. The United States has not yet undergone the real communications revolution that is on the way.

But some might say that there is a contradiction between sacrificing everything to maintain the competitiveness of our advanced industries and technologies and directing a larger proportion of our population into these new service activities, which do not seem to be profitable in themselves. It is precisely this contradiction that calls for innovation and the spirit of enterprise. We will never succeed in resolving the problems of employment, the quality of life, communications, and culture by using bureaucratic methods. The time is long past when Galbraith could convince most of his fellow economists that all the imbalances of an affluent society would be resolved by improving social services. It is clear now that neither the state nor public agencies can create the necessary jobs or satisfy the most desperate needs except at an outrageous cost, one that threatens seriously to reduce our competitiveness. Only radical innovations will make it possible for us to succeed. And if we are able to look at reality closely, we can see that society already reacts more positively to the problem than do politicians or intellectuals.

Inventing a New Type of Management

To adopt the strategy of the new service revolution, we must first abandon the paralyzing idea that says that new services, because they are a necessity for society, should be provided by public agencies or by local government because they can easily create jobs for the unemployed in these areas. No society, however rich, can solve the problem of creating jobs by using the bureaucracy. Neither the United States nor England has succeeded in this. The most that can be done is to give allowances to the unemployed, but administrative blindness can never seriously address itself to needs that it does not see. Even its response to deeply felt needs, such as education and, particularly, health, is so inadequate that it results in an unbearable inflationary spiral. It is frightening to realize that in spite of the immense growth of expenditures on health, the life expectancy of citizens is hardly increasing, and that in any society the relation between these expenditures and their results is less and less clear. Society can no longer bear the indefinite increase of these expenditures, any more than it can get caught up in similar spirals in other areas where the bureaucratic emergence of needs leads inescapably to the recognition of rights, and hence to an uncontrollable growth.[2] In the case of French society, which is at least as threatened in its competitive capacity, any increase in public expenses of this sort leads quickly to a society's being saddled with an unbearable weight. The weight of taxation is too strongly resented for everyone to be paid through taxes. Therefore, the payments by businesses have to increase directly or indirectly, for otherwise the financial deficit of the state becomes uncontrollable. Let us not forget the revolt of the California taxpayers, which imposed a sharp limitation of all services on the state government.

However, if public power cannot create jobs as it pleases, the capitalist market economy, as it is currently functioning, is totally incapable as well. And here we must get rid of another commonly accepted idea that is just as harmful. The problem is not the market, which is still reponsible for calling forth new needs at the same time as the means for satisfying them; rather it is that of the management of production and relations with the customer. The application of Taylorian management, which we have not yet gotten rid of in the traditional service area, is truly catastrophic when used in the new services. It either leads to an inflation of costs, or to a deterioration of quality, or to these two problems at the same time. If the activity is taken over directly or indirectly by public authority, the development of an inflationary spiral is inevitable. With a truly private activity, producers will take themselves out of the market because of costs that are too high or quality that is too low. Then what appears is the growth of vicious circles: inefficiency leads to a reduction in demand, which leads in turn to a Taylorian tightening of organization, meaning an even greater reduction in quality. The extraordinary dysfunctions that can be seen in activities that are managed by the public sector, such as education or health, are by no means absent from the private sector. But there they simply lead to a business failure, to drastic reductions in activity, or at least to the abandonment of plans for expansion. In 1970, Chris Argyris did a remarkable study of the vicious circles in an American consulting firm, whose management methods (to obtain the profit that they were able to calculate) led to the progressive reduction of their field of activity and the efficiency of their service.[3] This analysis made it possible to predict the serious problems that these firms would undergo in the United States as well as in Europe. In France, some of them met with even more dramatic disasters.

What is remarkable in the area of new services is the diversity of practices and results. The best and the worst coexist, with cost differentials that go from the ordinary to double or triple. This is because the problems of management presented by the new services are totally different from those presented by the traditional areas of management. They demand a new way of thinking. What is sold in this type of activity is not really a product or even the satisfaction of a need. It is help, a collaborative effort that will help the customer to change. The buyer is the real producer. As such, he is part of the organizational system of the service's activity. This activity cannot be understood without including the customer in it as an active element. This is clear in the case of education, even though it is not always easy to make people admit that it is the student who learns, who makes use of the teacher, and not the teacher who distributes his knowledge to passive consumers. The real results of this have not yet become apparent. But the same is also true of the health system, in which the sick person is not just a consumer of medicines or a passive object in the hands of a mechanic, but in most cases must be the active agent of his own cure, with the doctor only an adviser. And all recreational, cultural, and even communications activities require, in order to be renewed and expand, that the service provided stop being identified as a standardized consumption subject to traditional marketing techniques.

The success of the Club Mediterrannée is due to the fact that its founders understood this essential characteristic of the service that the recreational businessman is selling. The club does not consider its customer to be a consumer. What is sold to him is basically the possibility of living in a different way, thanks to the sea and sun, but also to the arrangements, expertise, implicit rules, and the social games that the club invented. The "gentil membre" (i.e., a "nice member") is also sold the services of the employees, the "gentils organisateurs," but in a totally different fashion from that of traditional hotels. The GOs are not the servants of the GMs; they do not exchange their subordination for a salary. They benefit from very substantial advantages, their social contacts, in their style of life, of learning, and even of leadership. Without this, their contracts would not be advantageous in strict money terms. An original management method goes with this system, which consists of the personal contribution of Gilbert

Trigano, the manager, and which is at least as financially rigorous as classical management systems but rests on radically different organizational principles.

Taylorian management is based upon breaking all activities down into the simplest possible steps, which can be standardized but must later be put back together. True, the art of management has never been reduced to the simple adoption of Taylorism. But as Herbert Simon, and later Russell Ackoff, among others, have shown very well, the managerial way of thinking has never entirely succeeded in getting free of this framework, which is extremely difficult to replace in the area of production, in spite of the very heavy human costs it imposes on workers. Moreover, for management, the bureaucratic system, particularly the one we are familiar with in France, constitutes an original version of this model, but one that is entirely recognizable, sometimes even caricaturing some aspects of it.[4]

In the new services, management must be based on radically different principles. It can tolerate neither fragmentation nor standardization but rests on an analysis of the resources of human material, which is characterized by an interdisciplinary approach, by adaptability and the possibility of growth. Its aim is to create the necessary sociological conditions for small, living social communities to form around supply of a service and for them not only to remain open but to be capable of setting up an intensive interchange between them and the outside, particularly the professional, world. To do this, intellectual models must be brought to bear, and a sufficient level of innovation maintained through constant research. Of course, management must be capable of profitably managing a diversity that should be a source of richness and not of disintegration. The revolutionary idea of the entrepreneur in this kind of sector will no longer be primarily a technological breakthrough, a new product, or even a new principle of organization but social innovation. Of course, enterprise will often depend on technological innovation. For example, computers will play a decisive role in this area, as well as many technological innovations that will appear in the area of communications. But none of these steps by itself will carry with it a new type of social organization. It is even possible to predict that there will be serious setbacks wherever people are unable to invent modes of cooperation and styles of management that allow them to benefit from technological progress.

A Strategy for New Development

The new service revolution has no chance of succeeding in time and of replacing our old, exhausted method of development unless it is simultaneously humanly enriching and practically profitable. This difficult contradiction requires innovation and the entrepreneurial spirit. We must find styles of organization and models for human relations that can get us out of the vicious circle of dehumanization and inefficiency in which we are now enmeshed. This is not an impossible task. There are already scores of examples in the areas of recreation, education, business services, and even commerce. For recreation, we can cite experiments as diverse as the Club Mediterrannée and the sailing club at Glénans. In commerce, similar characteristics show up, as we have seen in the revolution in market structure of truck farmers in St. Pol-de-Léon carried out by Alexis Gourvennec or the experiment of Jean Paquet, a baker from Clermont-Ferrand, who succeeded in totally transforming the system of human relations by which his profession lived in the rural area of central France.

In education, we can take the case of the organization "Retravailler," which was conceived and established by Evelyne Sullerot to give women who had to go back to work (or who wanted to after years outside the professional world) the intellectual and psychological capacity to do so. Here again, we find a new mode of organization in which those who are taught are really part of the system and who play an active role in it. In a way, each is not so much the raw material for the others as the support they need for growth. What the organizers provide is an organizational system as well as a way of thinking that is simple and practical but which represents an original intellectual contribution. The whole system is simultaneously human, efficient, and extraordinarily inexpensive, considering the results. A bureaucratic arrangement would take care of the same number of people at at least three times the cost, with doubtful results.

All of these examples suggest to me the outline of a strategy based on four elements: the development of a capacity for differentiating among individuals, situations, and arrangements; investment in knowledge; the use of human resources that until now have been neglected; and finally the total rejection of the bureaucratic model of management.

The capacity of human beings and social units to differentiate, to take care of things case by case—meaning that each case is tailor made—is both an aim and a means of action. A strategy for the development of the new service sector should be based on a recognition of this fundamental priority. I do not want to make a theory out of it but simply say that that is the direction in which we should be looking. The technological revolution from which modern heavy industry was born was based on standardization and uniformity. The new technology will allow us to change this pattern radically but only as long as we clearly understand that the problem is primarily human rather than technical and that we must choose to experiment in new areas—the area of new services—where we are not hampered by the past.

Another priority is investment in knowledge. In this case success does not lie only in a technological gamble but in a gamble on human capacities. Without a serious investment in knowledge growth cannot take place. We have to understand human systems that are infinitely more complex than the systems of objects of previous industrial revolutions, and we have to find the means to get the participants to become active in the system that is to be built. This implies thought, research, and new thinking about the conditions, possibilities, and limitations of human learning. Only investment in knowledge will allow us to consider the problems of the quality of life and also the problems of quality alone, which we are constantly facing.

What resources will be available for such a strategy? What is needed first is innovators, entrepreneurs, but they cannot be built from nothing. A good strategy for development should not seek to favor innovators in high-priority sectors but to base itself essentially on human resources that have been neglected. No technical revolution has ever been carried out by the establishment. The first, the most difficult one, was born among marginal workers in workshops outside cities that were not hampered by guilds and regulations. For the most part, these were mechanics, village inventors who started the first industrial revolution, that of the English textile industry in the eighteenth century. And it was first successful in the cotton industry, a new industry that was not included in the urban guilds.

Very often, however, say in education and health, the sectors of the new services are completely paralyzed by a long guildlike tradition. But elsewhere there are neglected human resources, above all those of young people and women, who are excluded in times of economic stagnation; they are the marginal workers of today's bureaucratic system. An active strategy of development must rely on them and be based on their aspirations. Remember my principle of the transformation of aspirations into a positive contribution for changing society. This phenomenon is already at work. This should not be surprising as far as the young are concerned since they have always been the agents of change. The revolutionary mystification of 1968 has partially sterilized a whole generation, but we are beginning to see more positive results; not all the marginal experiments were fruitless. The capacity to create has not weakened, it was just deformed. We have to free it more and to help it make its way.

As for women, who are also excluded from the system of the traditional professions, the hypothesis that they could play a more decisive role in the new service revolution may be surprising. Feminists generally favor an egalitarian point of view, which would exclude such a development. But I think there are two decisive arguments. First, regardless of the justice of the cause, feminists will almost certainly fail in their frontal attack on the professional system. The economic and demographic context is too unfavorable to them. The cost of creating new jobs of the same sort as present jobs would be exorbitant. Society has also begun to have trouble in bearing the extra demand for work by women, which has consequences for employment problems. No more-egalitarian distribution, which would necessarily be a bureaucratic one, can resolve the problem. The best chance that women have is the new service sector. Why should women not regard this as an opportunity? That is where everything is going to happen, where the world will be changing the most. Second, women have qualities and capacities that will be precious assets in this new area. Our culture has made them specialists in human relations, emotional arrangements, and caring for children, and this should no longer be considered as a sign of inferiority. It should be used as a resource; these qualities now will be opportunities for success.

The last element of a strategy for change is the dismantling of the traditional bureaucratic system. The progress that is possible in the areas of health and education is smothered by the weight of the administrative system that regulates these apparatuses. Costs are becoming prohibitive and results diminishing, and it is very difficult to change anything at all without changing everything at the same time. In these areas we have to prepare ourselves for tumultuous crises, but we should not be frightened by them. In other areas that have fortunately remained more free, the real problem is one of preventing the direct or indirect confiscation of successful activities by public authorities. The state, and even local and regional authorities, must learn to play a role in helping people to acquire knowledge, in counseling and indirect regulation, and must abandon their passion for control and regulation.

The Territories to Be Cultivated

I have already begun to give several examples of the new service revolution. I would now like to point out the general features of the areas included by this new frontier, from business services to recreation, and including communications, education, health, and culture.

It is important that up to now innovations have been most profound in the area of recreation, that is, in activities that are the most marginal in relation to the productive and administrative systems. I mentioned the case of the Glénans Sailing Club and the Club Méditerrannée, and there are scores of others. The results of these experiments are valuable not just for the area of recreation but for all sorts of other activities because the problem they solve is essentially the same: how the client and service user is to be made active, and how he is to be used to make the service more profitable and efficient.

The inventive genius apparent in the area of recreation could give just as remarkable results in cultural activities. Unfortunately the elitist system that was built up around culture, the aura of respect that defends it against the ignorant, has protected it against any such contact. Moreover, the patronage of the state and its monopoly over teaching have a stifling effect. It was predictable that the Cultural Centers and the Youth and Culture Centers, in spite of the spirit of many of their organizers, would only reinforce the vicious circle of noncommunication, which removes culture from the masses, and make it so expensive that it wastes away.[5] All the same, in spite of all obstacles, a new movement is already catching up with large parts of the population. The vogue of cultural organizations, of monument preservation societies, and folklore associations may make the professional esthetes smile, but it is a strong source of renewal. How are we to use this demand, which is also a supply of goodwill, to save and cultivate our national heritage, to improve the quality of life? It is not so much a problem of finance but one of imagination and thought. It is absurd to spend our time criticizing the truly sorry state of our heritage, of our monuments, of our cultural budget, if we can think only in terms of bureaucratic expenditures. The great German and English examples, to mention only the closest, should help us to think better.

There remains the basic blockage of our entire society due to the educational system, which not only sterilizes French culture but constitutes the most serious obstacle to the new service revolution. In discussing a possible strategy for opening up the elite and developing knowledge, I have suggested that we pass over the block of primary and secondary education; we will not succeed in getting things moving unless we have a more intense intellectual movement. I think that we will have to adopt the same wait-and-see strategy as with the new services. Education is certainly one of the cornerstones of the new service revolution, but public schools are in danger of being the last to be affected by it. The teaching world thrives on conventional ideas that are extremely conservative toward the sociological aspects of the teaching relationship, at the same time as it pretends to provide a view of the world that is progressive, if not revolutionary—as if the class, even one of twenty-five students, were a fundamental and intangible unit! As if the act of teaching must never be a person-to-person conversation between the students and the teacher! As if a school could never be anything but a bureaucratic community! As if the learning about human relations that a child will go through in this first community were not culturally more important than a good part of the course content given him! The response that has been tried for dealing with these problems, the counselling system for example, is a perfect bureaucratic response, and its failure has to be recognized. The same is true for the system of technical and vocational training, whose weaknesses in comparison to the German system, for example, explain much of the superiority of German firms in their organization of work.

What is most distressing is that there is still no real anxiety about these things. The world of education is closed in on itself and seeks only to protect itself from those who might threaten its monopoly—private education, adult education, agricultural training, business training, and the involvement of parents. The most important task of a responsible minister should be to work to change this behavior. Why cannot the traditional educational system realize that all of these areas that are outside it could be sources of renewal, free areas for experimentation? It is also time to make it take the first step toward change, to devote a reasonable part of its immense budget to research, particularly to understanding and evaluating activities that it is involved in.

Problems of public health have become matters of top priority all of a sudden because of the financial crisis of the social security system. The exponential growth of the expenses of the health system has begun to disturb governments and, gradually, the public itself. In contrast to the world of education, which has managed to remain stable in its splendid isolation, the world of health services is in crisis. Today we can no longer be content, as was done for so long, to make scapegoats out of the big pharmaceutical companies. The increase in expenses is primarily due to the inflation of costs entailed by the spectacular progress of technology, particularly advanced technology, to the difficulty of managing hospitals, and finally to the egalitarian bureaucratic workings of the social security system, which is not so costly in administrative expenses as in uncontrollable individual cases of waste. The overconsumption of medicine takes place within these workings. Pharmaceutical companies profit from it, of course, but it is absurd to hold them responsible.

Under these conditions it would seem to be highly unrealistic to look for a source of jobs and development in an area where costs make it less and less economical. Not only can individuals no longer pay for it, but the whole society is less and less able to deal with it. If inflation is destroying an immense potential market, is it not time to reconsider the system, or at least to experiment with new directions? It is the technocratic model of medicine that is in crisis rather than the demand for health services. The real phenomenon that should concern physicians is the gap that they allowed to grow between them and the rest of society. The general practitioner of the past had a human influence, a reputation that certainly made a notable out of him and also made him an adviser. He was a sort of missionary who relied on knowledge that he had gained from respected scientists. The general practitioner today has to treat his patients on an assembly-line basis and has become a simple dispenser of medicines. And yet there is so much ignorance to be countered among the general public, which needs to understand drugs far more than take them. What mistakes, what small and great anxieties could be avoided! There is a need for concrete, human advice that is essential to the quality of people's lives!

I think it would be better to think much more deeply about the contribution that the patient himself makes to medical activity. After all, it is he who cures himself with the help of the doctor, rather than the mechanical action of medicines that a computer could dispense just as well. Why could the general practitioner not become a sort of adviser, who with a good deal of work and organization would benefit from the tremendous value added by a well-managed group relationship? Let us take the simplest cases, pediatrics and geriatrics. The need for advice and the anxiety of mothers would be dealt with much better by group education in which the mothers would take an active role. And the need of the elderly for reassurance would be better satisfied by group interaction than by routine visits to the doctor's office. This is not an attack on one-to-one communication or on the freedom of patient and doctor; rather perhaps it is fundamentally an attempt to rid them of all their encumbrances. And more thought should be given to what they are starting to learn from the complex statistical analysis of the conditions under which many sicknesses appear. Research in these areas is still inarticulate, but it is enough to enable experimentation with the prevention of disease.

How can this transformation of the role of the local doctor be brought about? All sorts of formulas are possible, but I think that what is essential is that the possibilities for experimentation should be made available. For example, the social security system could deal with teams of doctors who take on the responsibility of education, prevention, and health for a sufficiently large number of customers (who volunteer to participate), providing there is a regular evaluation of the results. It might be objected that the largest expenditures are those incurred by order of specialists in hospitals. This is true, but these expenses will not be reduced by bureaucratic compression or even by standardization. What we do need is a health system that will cater to the basic human problems of patients and be capable of advising them and guiding them so that hospitals will be disencumbered and hospitalization time reduced. Moreover, let us not forget that in France, alcoholism is responsible for half of the expenditures for hospitalization.[6] This plague will not be beaten back by the heroics of advanced medical techniques, not by technocratic information, not by undifferentiated propaganda from the media, but by better control by individuals over their own problems. From this point of view, there would be an important role for medical workers and paramedics, whom society would much more willingly accept paying for if the relation between doctor and clients became warmer and if, moreover, the results were more convincing from the point of view of the quality of life. Then perhaps the specialist in advanced medicine could find his proper place again, which is elitist and not egalitarian simply because research and innovation are never very successful in a bureaucratic framework, which imposes a narrow conception of equality.

Finally, the area that is most open to the new service revolution, one where the success of a new type of development will be played out, is certainly that of communications. This is where the progress of technology is opening up the most extraordinary possibilities for change, directly with all the communications professions and indirectly to the extent that other areas, such as health and education, can be changed by new systems of communication. This is a case of human construction because technology alone does not hold the key to the problem. The complexity of the system of relations and changes that is needed to take advantage of the potential of technology is hard to grasp. It is not a question of making plans or even of creating a market but one of stimulating, step by step, the development of a network of interconnected markets, each working with the others. Think of the complexity of the system that was put into place in successive stages around the automobile: mass production, wholesalers, dealers, mechanics, gasoline distribution systems, gas stations, highways, transports, housing market . . . Such a system, once built, has its own logic and a formidable resistance to change.

Today's communications systems are fragmented and very complex. The communications revolution eventually will be carried out but it will require extraordinary efforts. This is because communication, leaving aside its economic complexity, is also a basic human phenomenon. It affects people in the most basic way; around and through it man becomes a social animal. In a narrow economic perspective, most of the time the consumption of information alone is considered. The development of mass media, essentially characterized by the power of the transmitter and the impossibility of feedback, which forces consumers to be passive, has clouded the issue. New technological progress is reintroducing the possibility of more human relationships, thanks both to the opening up of infinite choices and to the possibility of an active response by an increasing number of receivers. The possibilities of active involvement, of learning and discovery by everyone who wishes and has the minimum ability to do it, are immense. But at the same time they are an intolerable danger for the existing system of relations, and they will not be easily used. The paradox is striking: we spend our time denouncing technology that we fear will lead to the manipulation of people, while at the same time we are conditioned by a system that is blind but weighs very heavily on us. By pulling back before the possibilities of technology, we are actually maintaining the barriers that prevent us from freeing ourselves.

These complex systems will not function without relays, without intermediaries who will influence the choices within excessively open networks of relations. This is where jobs will appear, where the entrepreneurial spirit must be most active. And here, too, the struggle will be hardest against the bureaucratic model, which in this area is quintessentially a model of manipulation. Here again, the role of public authorities above all should be to invest in research, experimentation, the development of capacities for learning by consumers, and not to work out a priori juridical norms and regulations. Let me emphasize here to what extent we in France give too much importance to technology itself. Consider the question of access to information. Big machines are not important, nor are data banks, but data themselves are, meaning the capacity for gathering, analyzing, and using data. If we are in danger of depending on the Americans in this matter, it is not because of their technological lead but because of their intellectual lead, which is the only thing that will have made it possible for them to build up data banks of much higher quality than anything that we have been able to put together.

New Services and Society

But how can all these new services be paid for? For a long time now, it has been recognized that the size of the tertiary sector in France is too large, considering our industrial development.[7] We have an occupational distribution that is closer to that of the United States than that of Germany, one that is too large in relation to our level of development. And we have seen that there are too many executives and white-collar workers in our industry, compared to Germany. In fact, French development until now has been accomplished with an abnormally swollen and relatively parasitical tertiary sector. This peculiarity is related to the maintenance of social power by the middle classes, as much to the predominance of the state bureaucracy as to archaic systems of distribution and speculation. The strategy of the new services might then seem to run the risk of increasing even more the inflation of an unproductive tertiary sector. In fact this would be true if it were a question of creating jobs in public administration or in sectors that were protected and dominated by the civil service. But the strategy I am suggesting implies tactics of quite another nature, of which the principal one is as follows.

It means first using the strategy of developing new services based on the capacity of the users themselves to pay for them directly. If the productivity of these new services increases and if their quality improves at the same time, they will find takers. In fact, what the new technology brings us is the reduction of the difference in productivity between the tertiary and the secondary sectors. This may seem paradoxical, but this is what we have to depend on when we create new jobs. If we were to apply the potential of these technologies according to some bureaucratic diagram, we would reduce even more the number of jobs and, for an increase that was theoretically large but in fact small in relation to the whole system, we would excessively increase the cost of the necessary human quality demanded by the consumer.[8] If, on the other hand, we use these potentials to improve quality first, playing on the people's capacity for development as participants and not just as consumers, we can succeed simultaneously in creating jobs and making consumers pay for them if they are sufficiently involved to pay the cost of quality. Then the cost to society would remain relatively small, essentially linked to research and experimentation.

The second gamble is social. It is too easy to blame populist movements such as Poujadism to make a scapegoat out of the shopkeeper or artisan, only subsequently to see that when there is an unemployment crisis the class of artisans can absorb a great deal of manpower that consumers would be willing to pay for if they were deprived of efficient services. No drastic intervention to get rid of or reduce social groups considered to be out of date has ever succeeded, except in the case of bloody revolutions, with damaging results.[9] The social tactic implied by the strategy of the new social services is one of reorienting these middle classes. They may well be considered partially parasitical from the point of view of the social system as a whole, but this should not lead us to neglect the considerable assets of their members' ingenuity, activity, and initiative. The strategy of the new services means proposing new activities for superfluous officials and shopkeepers, activities that often are also in line with their wishes. In what is interpreted as marginalization, some of the young are instinctively looking for solutions among these technologies and new ways of life.

The third gamble is intellectual. The strategy of the new services means providing the means for learning and experimentation in radically new areas and therefore calling into question the accepted ideas that reign in traditional sectors. For example, I think that the management of industrial activities will be even more deeply shaken during the years to come by the experience of new services than it has been over the last twenty years by the pressure of competing foreign models because management, from a certain point of view, is itself a service activity, and even one of the new services. It is basically an activity involving human relations, deeply dependent upon a good system of communications. What we will be learning about systems of communication and education, or even about recreation, will certainly be useful for the renewal of high technology activity. Our international competitiveness will certainly be improved by this.

Can French society commit itself to such ventures? Nobody can guarantee this in advance. But I personally believe that the conditions for a renewal are there and that vast potentials are being ignored and wasted by an administrative and political system that refuses to understand the extent of the changes that are going on. The creative ferment has not disappeared in France; far from it. Even aside from all our industrial successes, many social creations have appeared over the last thirty years.

I have already mentioned the success of the farmers of Champagne and of the Léon region. They have not accomplished this miracle by following state guidelines and by asking for government subsidies. They have done it because they were able to take advantage of the progress of technology and agricultural biology in one case and of the organization of markets in the other. And they were able to do it because they had the courage, through the young farmers' movement, to undertake the tremendous job of mutual instruction that very quickly bore fruit. Not all French farmers succeeded as did those of Champagne or the Bretons of Gourvennec. But French agriculture, which seemed to be out of date and unchanging, was transformed at a social and economic cost much lower than in many countries, even the United States. Remember the human cost of the agricultural disasters of the 1920s and 1930s, described in *The Grapes of Wrath* by Steinbeck, and which did not save the American Treasury Department from spending billions of dollars in market subsidies.

Why should other areas of French society not be able to do as well? At the beginning of the 1950s, no expert had foreseen the successes of French agriculture. Their faulty analysis stemmed from their ignorance of the human factor, of the capacity of the French peasantry to awaken and take its affairs in hand. Why should the new services not provide the French with the opportunity for a similar resumption of control over their own course of change?

11
BY WAY OF CONCLUSION:
THE RESPONSIBILITY OF THE INTELLECTUALS

There is no successful change without innovation and without people fully assuming their responsibilities. There is no innovation without a strategy, and no strategy without thought. There is no choice without intelligence. If France has difficulties, if the French made poor choices, this is not because of its lack of coal, as used to be said, and not because of the management gap that was so dear to Jean-Jacques Servan-Schreiber, but because of intellectual backwardness. In all of the problems, I have pointed out that feasible strategies seem possible, and substantial resources can be brought to bear. But to enact these strategies, or others that are even better adapted, two preliminary problems always come up. We must be able to recognize the facts and be able to change our way of thinking.

More than any other social and professional group, French leaders and intellectuals should think about their responsibility in this respect. Very often they like ideas, which gives them the appearance of being intelligent. But they never really take them seriously, and they prefer to avoid taking risks. In today's world, a world of science and change, this aristocratic amateurism is out of date. Ideas have become a serious matter, and action has become an intellectual adventure.

What matters, and will matter more and more, is not ideas, opinions, and theories that are still pretexts for making speeches but the capacity for finding new ways of thinking, for presenting problems based on facts, and for trying out solutions. The task of intellectuals is to carry out this transformation; nothing is more important or more difficult. If this were impossible, then my own speech itself would also be utopian. But it is not necessary to hope in order to begin, nor is success necessary for us to persevere. In this regard, another book would be necessary. I will only present several remarks by way of conclusion.

1. Theories do not change the world. The most they can do, like tornadoes or whirlwinds that flatten human constructions in a single moment, is to help to destroy. Nor does the blind interaction of productive forces or the class struggle change the world. Nothing is done without the work of man, without his will, his hope, his responsibility. True, he labors without knowing where he is going. True, he deceives himself and does the opposite of what he wanted to do. But slowly he always surpasses himself. What makes change possible is the tools man fashions for action, which in the final analysis are ways of thinking that permit him to take control over things and over himself. It is what, from the perspective of past history, appears in the form of culture. In our advanced societies, the care of these tools has been more or less taken over by people called intellectuals, the official or officious guardians of our past culture and the beacons of our future culture.

2. There once was a time when guardianship of culture was a glorious function, one that was honored and hardly questioned, because changes were slow and it was more important to preserve than to increase the treasure. New practices were worked out gradually, and they entered the storehouses of the temple only after the event. True, the guardians always argued about the value of the items. Some worked on them in a useful way and others even made new ones. Still others awaited the great renewal. This idea frightened them but fascinated them at the same time. And sometimes a deep renewal (a new paradigm) really did succeed in emerging from the accumulation of practice and work, which at least partially threw the treasure into turmoil and made

it possible to overcome obstacles, to resolve problems that until then had been insoluble, to give a new enthusiasm to human endeavor.

3. But this time of conservatism, when culture was a treasure, is long since out of date. Culture has entered into everyday life, and it is to be expected that the man of culture will be called into question. True, there will always be a place for retreat into the ivory tower, for flashes of solitary genius, and for elitism, in the avant-garde as well as in the rear guard. But a complex society needs other intellectuals, more and more of them, who can work more directly with the real world. The existence of this new race of intellectuals calls into question, perhaps indirectly but constantly, the sovereignty of traditional culture. The resulting cultural crisis is very deep, and the disarray of intellectuals confronted by it is a social phenomenon whose importance has not yet been sufficiently gauged. The greater role of intellectuals in social life does not mean an increase in their power, their influence, or their rewards but rather leads to a decline in their status. When the number of intellectuals increases, when the boundary between intellectuals and practitioners becomes difficult to find, the intellectual can no longer be honored as he used to be. When anyone can enter into the temple, a certain anxiety on the part of the simple priests is conceivable. On the other hand, there is a displacement of traditional intellectuals both by intellectuals of the world of action and by those from the world of communication, those of the media. The disarray of the intellectuals and their disordered reactions in the face of the crisis of culture are phenomena manifested in all developed countries. The aristocratic intellectual is outdated, devalued, and disputed. He is asked to play a role in society and eventually is held responsible. Then he rears back, or more often he himself passes over to the opposition, with a vengeance. Like the simpleton Gribouille, he throws himself into the water so that he will not get wet. The

aristocrat becomes a demagogue. The young bourgeois intellectual goes beyond the proletarian on the Left.

4. French society, which has always given particular importance to intellectuals—Tocqueville is an example—was necessarily deeply affected by this crisis. May 1968 was the expression of this. A new wind seemed to be blowing, and people thought that they had made a blank slate out of the past. They were not far from burning books in order to find the answers in praxis. There were to be no more differences, no more teachers: the cultural community, housewives included, would finally succeed in squaring the circle and bringing about the unity of mankind. The mania for protest or destruction unfortunately was to lead to the reappearance of our old demons. Every single person, Young Turk, Sectarian Maoist, proletarian extreme leftist, or simple Poulantzasite, presumed to dictate to the human race how it should act, with an arrogance worthy of any great aristocrat of the nineteenth century. In practice, the terror of the far Left did nothing but briefly stifle the ardor for change nourished by the most idealistic youth. The universities were rebuilt to be even more bureaucratic than before, and the maligned apparatus of the French Communist party grew substantially as a result. Politics has certainly taken a leftward turn, but the hope of the Common Program of the Left showed itself to be nourished by illusions, misunderstandings, and faulty thinking. People were waiting for Godot, and they are still waiting. The crazy years of antipsychiatry, of parricide, and the renewal of a Marxism whose virginity is constantly being rediscovered, have left us with nothing but the taste of ashes and announced nothing but the return of a poor man's liberalism and a third-rate "new philosophy."

5. *Destroy, She Said*: The title of a novel by a famous avant-garde writer, Marguerite Duras, haunts me as I write these lines. Mar-

guerite Duras has a great deal of talent, and I have respect for her work. But like so many other intellectuals, she has set herself to cut and tape the wounds of a bourgeoisie that is still in the process of dying, a dying man who is the concern only of his torturer. Have we not sufficiently worked over the ground of noble fathers and pretentious people, the infinite varieties of hypocrisy, slaves who are the makers of their own chains? Have we not sufficiently denounced the failures of our era? In the final analysis, have not all eras failed as much as ours has? And this craze for denouncing, for exploding, for pillorying is just as absurd as the traditional search for a scapegoat. Who will be the scapegoat? Who will serve to justify our lack of power: the bosses, the priests, or the bourgeois? Is it not time to build, to apply the mind's resources to understanding the world, to think about the possibilities that it holds, about the resources that await there and that could be exploited? Is it not time to declare that if good literature does not make good sentiments, still less is it made with bad ones?

6. Far be it from me to want to regiment intellectuals. The ivory tower is not necessarily useless, nor is research on written expression, except that it is necessary to blow on it a little to get rid of the dust that gathers there. And why should there not be a little indignation, after all? There are still many sore points to be touched on in society, which is still too narrow. And we must accept the idea of revitalizing conventional ideas that have become outdated. But, I ask again, is it not time for intellectuals to build things up as well? I do not mean that they should be involved in politics or demand responsibilities but that they should apply their minds to social reality and to the people who breathe with such difficulty under its constraints. Is it not time to set out on an adventure, not of the armchair variety but one involving experimentation that takes place in the real world? Is it not time

to give up the denunciation of a culture that is our past—and the past cannot be changed—so that we can finally struggle with our way of thinking and change it?

The world is changing and with it our ways of thinking, and it would seem that intellectuals, French intellectuals at any rate, cannot see this. All they seem able to do is to denounce what mankind has had to suffer in the historical "process," and what it will still have to suffer if the forces of evil are unleashed.

But for man to suffer no more, he must be given the tools for thought that will permit him to understand and become active. Do not tell me that Marxism, or far leftism, or ecologism, or even liberalism are such tools for thought. These are theories of society, nothing more. Men do not need theories of society, meaning ideologies, but rather more practical means for thinking about what they do, a better understanding of the boundaries and limitations of human activity, and finally (and above all) they need to reorganize their freedom and therefore their responsibility.

Will we be able to respond to this new challenge, to forget the appearances and illusions of speech making and return to reality? We do not suffer from any particular curse. French society is not as infected by the "French disease" as our elites say and think. The intellectual or governing elites would do better finally to find the courage to bring about their own interior revolution. Their job is not to disturb society but to make it possible for all potential innovators in society to make their efforts at moving ahead.

TRANSLATOR'S POSTSCRIPT

Languages express the realities of the societies from which they issue, and sociological language is no different. I would like to explain several French terms employed by Crozier and have arranged them as themes that represent underlying patterns in French society. They include the relation between the ideas of technocracy and self-management, of knowledge and experimentation. I will also discuss the import of Crozier's concepts of strategy and investment.

In its simplest sense "technocracy" refers to the power of technicians, which tends to increase with the development of advanced technology in postindustrial society. Important decisions are more and more left to those who have specialized knowledge, whether of technology, planning, or management. For some this is a sinister development; technocracy can become a threat to democracy because social choices are not made by elected representatives but by experts who are not responsible to the people.

This observation could refer to the growing power of technicians in any advanced society, but technocracy in France is stronger and more controversial. This is so due to the highly centralized nature of the French state and the character of the top civil servants trained to exercise its power. The latter are a rigorously selected and exclusive elite, amounting to a technocratic caste, who enjoy immense social prestige and legitimacy. Due to the concentration of power in the executive branch under the Fifth Republic, this elite, always powerful in France, has become even more so in the last twenty years.

The French state is centralized as is no other in the West. It is not too much of an exaggeration to say that no significant political decisions can be made without consultation with the central government or its representatives, and the degree of centralization is still growing. There was a period of temporary and mild decentralization during the Third Republic, to which Crozier refers, but the process of centralization speeded up after the administrative reforms following World War II.

Thus not only is power passing more and more into the hands of a technically trained elite, this power is being concentrated in Paris. Technocracy for many Frenchmen means that distant, unelected, and irresponsible officials have the power to make far-reaching decisions that are bolstered by the legitimacy of the state.

Not surprisingly, there has been resistance to this phenomenon. In general it has taken two forms: the demand for decentralization and the demand for workers' control of industry. The first has taken several guises. During much of the nineteenth century it showed itself as conservative opposition to the consequences of the Revolution and the supposedly radical power entrenched in Paris. Federalism, which appeared as an organized political movement shortly before the turn of the century, was a conservative ideology. In the more recent past ethnic minorities, such as the Bretons and Corsicans, have added an autonomist or separatist tone to the call for reduction in the central government's power. With its policy of regionalization, the government established 22 regions in France, primarily for economic planning. But this has not decentralized power, it has merely deconcentrated it, allowing it to be exercised at a lower level by the regional prefect. He is still chosen by Paris, and his relation to the departmental councils and the mayors of communes is no different from before. This explains the radical nature of Crozier's recommendation for a regional assembly by universal suffrage.

While a convincing argument, it goes against centuries of political tradition.

While calls for decentralization have been frequent and of long standing, a related idea has recently come into vogue, that of *autogestion*, which I have variously translated as "self-management" or "workers' control of industry," depending on the context. If decentralization means the devolution of political power in Paris to localities, *autogestion* means the devolution of economic power from managers to workers. Widely debated, the idea found its way into the Common Program of the Left. The Program contained many heterogeneous elements, among which were the paradoxical nationalization of whole sectors of industry and the transfer of power over these industries to the people who worked in them. As Crozier explains, the inherent contradiction between these two steps would have led to a vast increase in state power and little practical change in the way factories were run. As such, self-management of industry by workers remains a fantasy. Fantasy it may be, but its strength must be understood in terms of the technocracy against which it was and is a rebellion.

Crozier places a great deal of emphasis on *connaissance* and *expérience*, the former denoting empirical knowledge and the latter both experience and experimentation. In a strategy for social revitalization, stressing the need for precise knowledge and for experimental programs might not be considered daring or innovative to the English-speaking reader, but in the French context these two ideas are extremely radical. A chief consequence of administrative centralization is that it leads to a division of labor between the core and the periphery. The former is given the job of making decisions, while provincial administrators carry them out. The basis for this division of labor is the belief that only the central administration can define what is in the general interest and work out an appropriate method of action; they alone can rise above local particularisms. As a consequence local and regional administrators are familiar with the everyday realities of applying rules and laws, while at the top administrators are closed off from reality, often quite unfamiliar with and not responsible for the practical effects of their decisions. This state of affairs is turned into a virtue; as one top civil servant put it, "In the final analysis, the best decisions are the ones that are made when one is able to be at some distance from reality." The reader may have been surprised to learn, for instance, that there is no research department worthy of the name in the French educational system and that this lack is viewed with equanimity by those at the top. The distance from reality that is typical of decision-makers underscores the innovative nature of what Crozier is suggesting, that administrators be brought into contact with everyday reality and the consequences of their decisions.

The authority of the central administration is exercised through rules, detailed and strict rules that attempt to be comprehensive. To make them comprehensive, an effort is made to foresee all possible situations that might apply. Naturally, this is impossible and leads to the maze of exceptions that always crops up when executives are attempting to apply the rules in concrete situations. The essence of the rule-making process is that it is highly logical and deductive. The idea of having an experimental program, tried for a limited period of time to see if it works and how it might be modified, goes totally against the spirit of the top civil service's mode of operation.

The title of this book in French is *On ne change pas la société par décret*, or "You cannot change society by administrative fiat." Yet this is exactly how the government has been striving to change French society, with comparatively little success, as the author argues. The true import of what Crozier is suggesting is underlined by the deductive and fact-free context in which these administrative fiats have traditionally been formulated. Knowledge and experimentation are urgently needed, but they have fundamental implications for how the French civil service must change its ways.

The reform of education, administration, taxation, the distribution of incomes, and numerous other systems has been a topic of discussion and occasionally of action since the sense of renewal that followed the Second World War. But reform is always carried out from the top, and those at the top are generally unaware of what is going on in everyday, practical life. All-encompassing and logically deduced rulings cannot take into account practical circumstances, and in the final analysis it is therefore impossible for an administration to reform itself by fiat.

This leads us to the originality of the approach to reform that Crozier is urging, which is based on the related concepts of strategy and investment. These terms have an explicitly military ring to them, the first referring to choices of weak points in the system where pressure can be brought to bear to effect change and the latter referring to investment in both the financial sense of choosing how to obtain a return on limited resources and the tactical sense of investing an enemy position to be taken. Crozier proposes a kind of guerrilla warfare of social change, attacking the enemy not at his strongest points but only at his weakest, where success is assured. He opposes this approach to that of the technocrats, whose favorite program has been reform, and to that of the Marxists, whose favorite program has been confrontation of the capitalist system as a whole. Both of these approaches hold out little practical chance of success because they suffer from a holistic approach to social problems.

The importance of using guerrilla tactics for bringing France into the latter part of the twentieth century is pointed out by the meaning of another social fact that Crozier discusses, that of social claims or social demands. The role of claims and demands in social conflict in France explains the stalemated nature of the relationship between hostile social groups. Social demands constitute the exact opposite of strategy and investment because they are part of a pattern of confrontation and mistrust—between classes, regions, ideologies, and, more recently, generations—that historically has kept groups frozen in postures of fruitless hostility. This leads to the passion for destruction that obsesses revolutionaries, which is so similar to the holistic social engineering dear to the technocrats: both ignore the delicacy of the human stuff with which they are working. The making of extravagant demands has to be made into a source of movement rather than a source of immobility. This explains the urgency of Crozier's call for translating demands into resources for change, particularly the demands of women and the young. Unless this is done, one can easily foresee the latter two groups falling into positions of sterile opposition.

Technocracy and self-management; knowledge and experimentation; strategy, investment, and social demands—all are terms whose meaning in English is quite different from their significance in the French context. To the English-speaking reader many of Crozier's arguments (such as the need for empirical studies in education and the need for cross-fertilization among the elite training schools, the universities, and the National Scientific Research Council) would at first seem self-evident. But the underlying meaning of the terms I have described explains the immensity of the task he is calling for, given the structural realities of France. The explanation of these realities should serve to convey the originality and daring Crozier shows in both his analysis of what is wrong with French society and his strategy for bringing France into the postindustrial age.

NOTES

Chapter 1

1. In May 1968 French society was shaken by a student upheaval that triggered a quasi-revolution.

2. At the very moment when those in the media have such great power in political and social questions, some of them would like to prohibit public opinion polls. Polls do have defects, but isn't it better to be informed by the existence of a real fact—the percentage of voters who intend to vote in a certain way—than the prejudices or presuppositions of some commentator, who quickly becomes an influence over how people think? What must be eliminated is the biased or superficial opinion poll.

3. But in some other, narrowly technical areas, as in aerospace, successes have been spectacular. The successes of NASA show that Babel can be overcome.

Chapter 2

1. Philip the Fair, at the beginning of the Fourteenth Century, and Napoleon Bonaparte are the first and the last in the chronology of scapegoats held responsible for French centralization.

2. Alain Peyrefitte, *Le mal français*, (Paris: Plon, 1977).

3. The American Army Corps of Engineers was patterned on the French model, but never attained such perfection.

4. One Frenchman, René-Victor Pilhes, wrote a recent bestseller with a very funny and improbable plot about the crumbling of a gigantic technostructure.

Chapter 3

1. What the French call *grandes écoles* (elite training schools) are equivalent in prestige to the top Ivy League law schools and medical schools, the engineering schools of the Massachusetts Institute of Technology, and the major business schools in the United States. The French system is far more elitist and exclusive, however.

Chapter 4

1. A traditional image of administrative absurdity is depicted in this play by an anarchist schoolboy in 1888. Ubu King is a tyrant whose main instruments are the Finance Pumping Engine and the "de-braining machine."

2. Ninety-four percent of farmers know people in positions of power and 84 percent think they have some recourse to them if they are in trouble. In contrast, an average of 50 percent of craftsmen, shopkeepers, white-collar, clerical, and sales personnel, and blue-collar workers know someone in power; those who think they have recourse in time of trouble are 60 percent. Concerning the administrative system, 62 percent of farmers are optimistic, compared to 39 percent of workers and 42 percent of craftsmen, white-collar and sales and clerical workers. See the report of Elie Sultan, in *Décentraliser les responsabilités: Pourquoi? Comment?* (Paris: La Documentation Française, 1976).

3. Pierre Grémion analyzes this extremely well in his book *Le pouvoir périphérique* (Paris: Seuil, 1977).

4. See the analysis by Pierre Grémion and Jacques d'Arcy, *Les Relations des services extérieurs du ministère de l'Economie et des Finances avec leur environnement départmental* (Paris: CSO, 1969).

5. Jean-Claude Thoenig, *L'Ere des technocrates: le cas des Ponts et Chaussées* (Paris: Editions d'Organisation, 1973).

6. See the analysis of Erhard Friedberg in *Ou va l'administration française?* (Paris: Editions d'organisation, 1974), pp. 101–140.

7. The massive investments in telecommunications should not make us forget the extraordinary lag we developed over twenty years, particu-

larly since the Nora-Minc report shows that telecommunications are the nerve center of the postindustrial world.

8. Telephone services in France are provided by a public agency.

9. Unlike the Swedish State Audit Office, which underwent an astonishing transformation and today is the main management consulting organization for the entire Swedish public administration system.

Chapter 5

1. DeGaulle had decided on a regional reform, but many of his followers, especially those loyal to Chirac, fought to maintain the "unity of the Republic."

2. We have already shown this in a study carried out for Alain Peyrefitte, who was then minister of administrative reform. See Elie Sultan, *Décentraliser les responsabilités: Pourquoi? Comment?* (Paris: La Documentation Française, 1976), p. 8.

3. The reader should be reminded that French communes are usually very small. A field officer of a Ministry as important as the Ministry of Equipment must cater to twenty or thirty such districts.

4. These figures are from Michel Crozier and Jean-Claude Thoenig, in ibid.

5. A canton is an administrative unit that has lost all meaning and importance. It is the equivalent of a county, but on a much smaller scale.

6. Although people are generally attached to this system, the number of elected officials who dare directly to defend this practice is fairly small: 8 percent of urban elected officials, 33 percent of elected officials in small and medium towns, and 47 percent of the elected officials in villages and rural hamlets. See ibid., p. 38.

Chapter 6

1. The Paris School of Mines is at the top of the elite engineering schools.

2. In French, these schools are known by the acronyms HEC, CESA, IEP (or Sciences-Po) and ENA, respectively.

Chapter 7

1. The proposal by Jacques Monod, *Le Hasard et al necessité* (Paris: Seuil, 1970), on this matter seems doomed to failure.

2. France is not alone in this case. The United States has become more and more the victim of such short sightedness during the last ten years.

3. Alexander Zinoviev's *The Radiant Future* is a strong caricature of this. Some aspects of French research resemble Soviet institutions.

4. This was written in the middle of a dramatic crisis in the French steel industry, and a similar one arose in the United States three years later.

5. The United States has very different problems in this matter. I have tried to discuss them in *Le mal américain* (Paris: Fayard, 1980).

6. Many formulas are possible to give secondary school students more choices. All advanced countries except France are experimenting in this area. I explained why I thought that even though the reform of the educational system is most important, it cannot be the first priority. This is entirely clear for a problem such as the choice of what courses to take. This reform would imply the total overthrow of the French school system because it cannot succeed unless the unity of a school and its administration is reinforced. It demands a capacity for cooperation among teachers that they refuse to show at the present time.

Chapter 8

1. But the American John Rawls gave it its most elaborate definition in *A Theory of Justice* (Cambridge, Mass.: Harvard University Press, 1973).

2. As the authors of *Profil économique de la France* put it, "Attempts at obtaining a regulation of the progression of taxes have proven to be even more difficult. Until now it has not been possible to enact an explicit policy of regulation and redistribution of incomes, for reasons that are as much technical (insufficient statistical knowledge of nonsalary incomes and the consequent impossibility of fighting against fiscal fraud) as they are political (resistance of the different parties involved against participation). (Paris: La documentation française, 1975).

3. The drought tax was a bill to help farmers hurt by the terrible drought of 1976; it imposed a surtax on higher incomes.

4. The Center for the Study of Incomes and Costs is a semipublic body whose extremely sophisticated studies on income distribution within occupational classes disproved much of the rhetoric on inequality of incomes. See their book, *Les Revenus des Français* (Paris: Editions Albatros, 1977).

5. Michel Crozier, *The Stalled Society* (New York: Viking Press, 1973).

6. Source: "Systèmes Cofremca de suivi des courants socio-culturels" MCA, 1977.

7. This is perhaps one weakness of the excellent book by Christian Stoffaes, *La Grande menace industrielle* (Paris: Calmann-Lévy, 1978).

Chapter 9

1. Le Monde is the newspaper read by the French liberal establishment.

2. See the survey in the *Quotidien de Paris* (July 1976).

3. M. Maurice, F. Sellier, and J. J. Silvestre, *Production de la hierarchie dans l'entreprise*, Lest, (Aix: 1977). Editions Clair-Obscur. This precise sociological study deals with a number of businesses that can be compared very closely.

4. Ibid.

5. Michèle Legendre, "Les Attitudes et le comportement des employés de bureau parisiens," *CORDES* (1978).

6. To be fair, I should add that this antiunion technical innovation was accompanied by a social transformation that was extremely radical: the complete equality of incomes between manual and intellectual workers.

7. COFREMCA poll, 1977.

8. Peter Drucker, *The Age of Discontinuity* (New York: Harper and Row, 1968).

9. McKinsey is a large consulting firm that has been very successful in France.

10. Norman MacRae, "The Coming Entrepreneurial Revolution," *Economist* (December 25, 1976).

Chapter 10

1. Simon Nora and Alain Minc, *L'Informatisation de la société* (Paris: La Documentation française, 1978). This book has been published in English in the United States (*The Computerization of Society*, MIT Press, 1980).

2. The phenomenon that is appearing in the United States is very unsettling. During a fairly long incubation period, the premiums were far smaller than planned because bureaucratic management cannot make the needs emerge; but then their increase became more and more rapid and created inflation.

3. Chris Argyris, *Participation et organisation* (Paris: Dunod, 1970). This book is a translation from the English.

4. Readers interested in this problem may refer to my *Le Phénomène bureaucratique* (Paris: Seuil, 1964), and to *L'Acteur et le systeme* (in collaboration with Erhard Friedberg) (Paris: Seuil, 1977).

5. These centers were two creations of the 1960s.

6. This is almost the same now in the United States.

7. See, for example, Daniel Malkin, "La tertiorisation de la société," in *Questions de la société tertiaire,* DATAR, Travaux de recherche en perspective, 1973.

8. The Swedish way of developing social services seems to have reached its limits, and I would tend to think of it as outdated. In spite of the much more favorable conditions of Swedish society, the general inflation of costs is a crushing social burden. Taxpayers revolt and consumers blame the bureaucracy.

9. Leftists should not forget that the hopes of socialists in Chile and Portugal were dashed by the resistance of these "archaic" middle classes, supposedly doomed by history: Chilean truck drivers and Portuguese small landowners.